# Lexical Profile of AI-Generated Content in Higher Education

# Linguistic Insights

Edited by Maurizio Gotti
Emeritus Professor,
University of Bergamo (Italy).

Volume 318



PETER LANG
Lausanne · Berlin · Bruxelles · Chennai · New York · Oxford

David Hirsh

# Lexical Profile of AI-Generated Content in Higher Education

PETER LANG

Lausanne · Berlin · Bruxelles · Chennai · New York · Oxford

**Bibliographic Information published by the Deutsche Nationalbibliothek**
The Deutsche Nationalbibliothek lists this publication in the Deutsche Nationalbibliografie; detailed bibliographic data is available online at http://dnb.d-nb.de.

**Library of Congress Cataloging-in-Publication Data**
A CIP catalog record for this book has been applied for at the Library of Congress.
LCCN number: 2025032717

ISSN 1424-8689
ISBN 978-3-0343-6121-7 (E-PDF)
DOI 10.3726/b23152
ISBN 978-3-0343-6113-2 (Print)
ISBN 978-3-0343-6122-4 (E-PUB)


Published by Peter Lang Group AG, Lausanne, Switzerland

info@peterlang.com



www.peterlang.com

# Contents

# List of Figures

# List of Tables

# 1. Introduction

In 1993, as a Master of Arts (Thesis only) student at Victoria University of Wellington under the supervision of Paul Nation, I engaged with early versions of Vocabulary Profiling programs designed to capture vocabulary use in written texts. My thesis titled *The Vocabulary Demands and Vocabulary Learning Opportunities in Short Novels* explored vocabulary use in three texts: *Alice's Adventures in Wonderland* written by Lewis Carroll published in 1865; *The Pearl* by John Steinbeck published in 1947; and *The Haunting* by Margaret Mahy published in 1982. The study was motivated by a desire to determine the vocabulary size required to read unsimplified texts as well as to investigate the opportunities presented in short novels such as these for learning of new words through repeated occurrences of these words in context.

The selection of the three texts spanned nearly 120 years of written language (1865 to 1947 to 1982) from authors located in the UK (Lewis Carroll), the US (John Steinbeck) and New Zealand (Margaret Mahy). They were written by authors widely respected and loved within their representative countries of setting. In this regard, collectively, the three short novels provided a snapshot of high quality modern English literature.

As for the Vocabulary Profiling program, two versions were developed by my former high school classmate Alex Heatley titled *Frequency* and *Range*. While Frequency provides a vocabulary profile of a single text, Range can be used to compare vocabulary use across texts. A core component of the vocabulary analysis is counting of word occurrences in a text based on pre-defined lists of words, termed *base-word lists*. The base-word lists I utilised were the first thousand and second thousand word lists derived from Michael West's (1953) *General Service List* (GSL), which was designed to capture the most useful 2000 high frequency words as a target vocabulary list for English as Second

Language (ESL) learners. The GSL was constructed based on written texts available at the time.

The base-word lists present headwords alongside other members of the word family. Along these lines, the following are counted as members of the same word family:

*help, helps, helped, helping, helpful, unhelpful*

The pedagogical thinking is that familiarity with one form will provide relatively easy access to other forms in the word family in terms of learning burden.

The study of the three novels carried out in 1993 captured patterns of vocabulary use in texts created by humans.

## 1.1 The GenAI Era

I joined the University of Sydney in 2007, teaching on the Master of Education (TESOL) degree program. Between 2007 and 2025, I observed minimal changes in the academic environment, although advances in Artificial Intelligence (AI) during this period had ushered in substantive new Generative AI (GenAI) applications in the 2020s. With the availability of Generative AI tools such as *ChatGPT, CoPilot, Gemini, Claude, DALL-E* and *MidJourney*, the University at the start of the 2025 academic year adopted a policy which reflected our collective views on appropriate and ethical uses of GenAI in learning and in assessment tasks.

The University made a distinction between use of GenAI as a learning tool, which is permitted with correct acknowledgement, and use of GenAI to produce written work which is falsely presented as the student's original work, which would breach academic integrity. The policy reflects the University's engagement with a changing world, and the desire to equip our graduates with the knowledge and skills to engage responsibly and ethically with GenAI in their future professional life.

As I read through the first batch of submitted assignments prepared under the new policy, and note the student declarations on use or non-use of GenAI in the preparation of their essays, I wonder what models of language use GenAI is exposing our students to. It seems worth asking the question: Has GenAI changed the nature of written language use? For me, as a vocabulary researcher, one research avenue for exploring the answer to this question will be found in comparing vocabulary use in GenAI texts with vocabulary use in texts written without use of GenAI. This is the focus of the current book.

## 1.2 GenAI in Higher Education

The current book thus investigates vocabulary use in GenAI texts with a particular interest in written content generated for academic or scholarly purposes. So what is GenAI content? The term Large Language Models (LLM) is used to describe applications of artificial intelligence (AI) which are programmed to both generate and understand human language. Thus, LLM can respond to a prompt such as *What is a black hole?* and then understand further related comments and questions on a discussion thread, providing tailored responses in a human-like conversational manner. Large Language Models based on datasets are the powerhouse behind GenAI applications involving language.

We can broadly view GenAI created content as the output generated by computer algorithms to a given prompt. The algorithms work with coded models based on patterns within large datasets of freely available published texts written by humans. The GenAI texts we see are products of a process of AI learning utilising these large datasets of human-written (non-GenAI) texts. Thus, these GenAI outputs can be viewed as mathematical models designed to produce meaningful human-like language. AI is still in relative infancy, if we appreciate its possibilities for development in the future.

GenAI texts generated for research purposes in higher education can be divided according to academic disciplines, such as arts, commerce, law and science. Within these disciplines, further distinctions can be made at the subject area level to reflect degree programs offered in the higher education sector. This accounts for expected differences in vocabulary use between, for example, engineering and architecture, sociology and anthropology, nursing and pharmacy. Within subject areas, texts (GenAI versus non-GenAI) representing areas of current interest can then be investigated. In this way, a basis is established to compare, for example, a published research article on *Prospects for Malaria Eradication in Sub-Saharan Africa* and GenAI content on the same topic. Such an analysis provides a snapshot in 2025 of how the fast-evolving GenAI technology is utilising and presenting vocabulary within scholarly texts generated.

## 1.3 Vocabulary Profiling

Paul Nation at Victoria University of Wellington commissioned Alex Heatley to develop computer-based programs for analysing vocabulary use in texts. Two versions were developed: *Frequency* and *Range*. Frequency was developed to capture word use in a single text, matching words used against base-word lists such as the first thousand words, the second thousand words, and the *University Word List* (UWL) (Xue & Nation, 1984). This program was used to analyse word use in Hirsh and Nation's (1992) study of vocabulary demands of reading short novels. Range was developed to compare word use across texts. This program enabled construction of Coxhead's (2000) *Academic Word List* (AWL). The software and a wide range of base-word lists are readily available for use through Tom Cobb's (2025) *Compleat Lexical Tutor* website. This book uses the term *Vocabulary Profiling* to refer to use of computer-based vocabulary analysis programs.

The output for a text analysed through Cobb's (2025) *Compleat Lexical Tutor* website displays word frequency in a text as *types* and as *families*. By types, we count the following word forms separately:

*help, helps, helped, helping, helpful, unhelpful*

By families, data on word frequency cover multiple members of the word family. Thus, we can see data on, for example, the percentage of word occurrences (i.e., tokens) in a text from the first thousand-word list (termed K1 words), the second thousand-word list (termed K2 words), and academic words, counted as word families.

The concept of *word families* groups together different forms of a word based on the following criteria: frequency, regularity, productivity and predictability. Collectively, these are designed to reflect a pedagogical principle that learning of one form of a word can provide relatively easy access to other recognisable forms of the word. For example, having learned the word *arrive*, adding to one's mental lexicon the forms *arrived, arrives, arriving* and *arrival* would not constitute a substantial learning burden. That is, learning new members of a word family is significantly easier than learning other words. Bauer and Nation (1993) devised seven levels for grading the learning burden of various derivatives and affixes. Paul Nation and other vocabulary researchers have utilised these levels to make principled decisions regarding how to classify word families for research, teaching, learning and testing purposes.

## 1.4 Vocabulary Lists

Before the advent of computerised programs designed to capture vocabulary use in texts, language teachers and researchers alike utilised largely manual means of identifying, classifying and counting word use. This led to development of lists of sub-technical (i.e., academic) words commonly used in academic discourse. As an example of this process, Praninskas (1972), Lynn (1973) and Ghadessy (1979) all sought to capture sub-technical (i.e., academic) words occurring in texts across a range of subject areas encountered by English as a Second Language (ESL) students in higher education. Campion and Elley (1971) similarly sought to capture such words to inform development of test materials used to assess overseas students for admission to New Zealand universities.

With the advent of computerised programs and corpora to assist in comparing vocabulary use across texts and to assist in listing words according to frequency and range of occurrence, new studies provided us with attempts to capture both academic and technical words used in academia. This included Xue and Nation's (1984) *University Word List*, Coxhead's (2000) *Academic Word List*, Coxhead and Hirsh's (2007) *Pilot Science-Specific Word List*, Ward's (2009) *Basic Engineering Word List*, Hsu's (2013) *Medical Word List*, and Matsuoka and Hirsh's (2018) *Specialised Vocabulary of High School Science*, to name a select range of such studies.

Computerised programs and corpora have also enabled development of word lists based on frequency of occurrence, at word levels, to provide, for example, a representation of the vocabulary use in the *British National Corpus* (BNC), the *Corpus of Contemporary American English* (COCA), and combined for BNC-COCA way beyond West's 2000 word GSL up to the 20,000 word level (see Nation, 2025). These lists have collectively provided students, academics, and research teams with a wide range of resources for vocabulary analysis and profiling of texts.

## 1.5 Anticipations of the Future

GenAI is still in its infancy yet evolving rapidly. There are a number of areas in which we can expect to observe developments in the future.

One of these reflects the linguistic diversity of the world we inhabit. An estimated 7159 languages are spoken in 195 or so countries (Eberhard et al., 2025). Some of these languages have very small numbers of speakers, while other languages have substantial populations. Some countries have afforded official status to multiple languages. To exemplify this, India, one of the world's more linguistically diverse countries, has afforded official status to 22 languages in addition to Hindi and English. These are: Assamese, Bengali, Bodo, Dogri, Gujarati, Hindi, Kannada, Kashmiri, Konkani, Maithili, Malayalam, Manipuri, Marathi, Nepali, Odia, Punjabi, Sanskrit, Santali, Sindhi, Tamil, Telugu, and Urdu (Khanuja et al., 2021).

We can assume that GenAI will accommodate the most widely spoken languages in the world. It is unclear how effectively GenAI will accommodate and reflect linguistic diversity beyond the world's more widely spoken languages. We can assume some languages with very small numbers of remaining speakers may be overlooked, although future developments in AI may provide a means to revitalise some endangered languages, and in the process allow future transmission of cultural and spiritual knowledge.

A second area we can expect to see further developments is the refinement of GenAI texts to disciplinary norms and expectations to increase the scope for GenAI texts to be of publishable standards. This will open the door for GenAI texts to be accepted as trust-worthy additions to the knowledge base on which we defer to for theoretical understandings and study findings. With this development, associated ethical concerns will be confronted.

A third area we can expect to see further developments is the incorporation of AI in human endeavours, as an integrated agentic model, in which AI actors or entities autonomously participate in processes of information identification, discussion, negotiation, deliberation, and enactment. To exemplify this, in fields such as medicine and engineering, AI incorporated decision-making and developments will likely become the norm.

As we move more confidently into the AI era and adjust to the opportunities and ethical challenges presented by new developments in the area of Agentic AI based on autonomously functioning AI systems, the current book provides one of many possible points of reference from 2025 to evaluate the direction and impact of AI developments.

# 2. GenAI in Higher Education

On November 30, 2022, the Artificial Intelligence (AI) company *OpenAI* based in San Francisco, California, released *ChatGPT* for free-of-cost research preview purposes. Enhanced subscription versions soon followed, in addition to free-to-use versions available through various digital platforms. While ChatGPT was not the first GenAI model, its launch had the distinction of marking a new era in generative artificial intelligence in terms of its widespread and public availability and functionability. Numerous other GenAI tools have similarly become available in the 2020s, including *CoPilot, Gemini, Claude, DALL-E* and *MidJourney*.

Then, on January 20, 2025, the Artificial Intelligence (AI) company *DeepSeek* based in Hanzhou, China, publicly launched *DeepSeek-R1*. Its model was seen as a competitive alternative to ChatGPT in terms of its open-source approach and efficient performance. Other GenAI tools developed in China include *Qwen2.5* and *Kimi 1.5*.

This chapter firstly introduces Artificial Intelligence (AI) and Generative Artificial Intelligence (GenAI) with explanations and exemplifications of key terms, before considering applications of GenAI in higher education.

## 2.1 Artificial Intelligence

Artificial Intelligence (AI) is a term used to refer to computers or machines which can perform tasks typically requiring human intelligence, including problem-solving and decision-making tasks (Oliveira & Figueiredo, 2024). We can see evidence of AI in computers which have been programmed to play chess. For this skill, the computers have gone through a process of training called 'deep learning' involving analysing vast amounts of chess moves and games to identify optimal strategies to win against an opponent. In this way, AI resembles, and can exceed, the reasoning, learning and actions of humans to perform tasks which mimic human-like behaviour.

Philosophers have pondered concepts around human versus artificial intelligence for thousands of years, with many documented attempts over time to create mechanised machines which operated autonomously (referred to as automata) of various forms in ancient civilisations (Dixon, 2004). Examples include mechanised figures, animals and chariots in ancient China, and small mechanical figurines in ancient Greece. One such example is a silver doll claimed to have human-like movements in the time of Aristotle. More recently, we have complex automated clock systems being developed in Europe from the thirteenth century onwards as well as artistic automata, termed Karakuri puppets, being developed in Japan between the seventeenth and nineteenth centuries.

When we talk of AI now, we tend to refer to a shorter history covering the twentieth and twenty-first centuries, to reflect technological advances with a direct link and developmental pathway to forms of AI and GenAI used today.

Some key pioneering developments in AI are in the areas of robotics, autonomous vehicles, and computers capable of playing board games against humans and other computers (Benko & Lányi, 2009). Key among these pioneering developments is the first industrial use of a robot called *Unimate* in 1961 on a car assembly line at General Motors, New Jersey. Unimate attended to transporting tasks deemed too dangerous for human workers. Then in 1979, an autonomous vehicle called the *Stanford Cart* developed at Stanford University displayed the capacity to autonomously traverse a room, avoiding objects.

From 1993 onwards, a robotic program was under development at MIT termed the *Cog Project* (Scassellati, 2019). The project was motivated by a concept of robotic learning through interaction with the world, replicating child developmental patterns and behaviour. The resulting Cog robot displayed a combination of mechanical robotics, perceptual systems to provide the robot with sensory capacity, and computational systems to promote autonomous learning. The Cog robot was able to imitate childlike behaviour and laid the groundwork for future autonomous robotic programs.

In 1997, a computer program termed *Deep Blue* developed by IBM played against and bet the world chess champion, Gary Kasparov, in a machine versus human match. By 2023, NASA was navigating the planet Mars with two autonomous rovers, *Spirit* and *Opportunity*.

**Table 2.1:** Key developments in AI

| Year | People or Technology | Focus |
|---|---|---|
| 1950 | Alan Turing's Turing Test | Proposes a test for machine learning which reflects the AI principle of mimicking human intelligence |
| 1955 | John McCarthy | Coins the term artificial intelligence |
| 1961 | Unimate | Pioneering industrial robot replacing humans on an assembly line |
| 1964 | Eliza | Pioneering chatbot developed at MIT capable of having conversations with humans |
| 1966 | Shakey | Pioneering human-like robot developed at Stanford capable of reasoning |
| 1974–1980: first AI winter representing an extended period of reduced AI funding and interest | | |
| 1979 | Stanford Cart | Pioneering autonomous vehicle developed at Stanford University |
| 1987–1993: second AI winter representing an extended period of reduced AI funding and interest | | |
| 1993 | Cog Project | A series of robots developed at MIT over a number of years |
| 1997 | Deep Blue | Pioneering chess-playing computer developed by IBM |
| 1998 | KISmet | Pioneering emotionally intelligent robot developed at MIT |
| 2002 | Roomba | Pioneering AI vacuum cleaner developed by iRobot |
| 2011 | Siri | Pioneering virtual assistant available on smart phones developed by Apple |
| 2022 | GPT-3 | Pioneering software released capable of natural language processing developed by OpenAI |

The history of AI has its ups and downs associated with increased and then decreased funding and associated developments. Two periods of notable reduced funding and developments are termed the *AI winters*. A summary of key developmental events in the recent history of AI (see Grzybowski et al., 2024) is represented in Table 2.1. The recent history reflects early developments and thinking in the 1950s and 1960s, followed by a revival and acceleration of developments from the late 1990s to now.

US military funding towards development of AI took the form of the *RAND Corporation* developed in 1948 and was tasked in its early days with aiding the US in its Cold War struggle with the Soviet Union in the 1950s and 1960s (Hounshell, 1997). Key advances shaped development of fighter jets, space exploration and a host of more civil applications.

For further explanations of AI, see Oliveira and Figueiredo (2024), Lee (2025), Phillips-Wren and Virvou (2025), and Prather et al. (2025).

## 2.2 Generative Artificial Intelligence

While we use the term Artificial Intelligence (AI) to refer to systems that replicate human intelligence, with a general focus on analysis and prediction, Generative Artificial Intelligence (GenAI) refers to specific uses of AI to generate new content such as text, images and sounds that are human-like (Oliveira & Figueiredo, 2024). This is based on learning patterns from vast datasets. The AI tasks performed reflect the types of data used to create the AI. Some key developmental stages in GenAI (see Al-Amin et al., 2024) are shown in Table 2.2.

Thus, if we are talking about GenAI in academic contexts, this refers to the capacity of AI to understand academic prompts and texts and create new content appropriate to the prompt. A prompt could be a question such as *What does Philosophy of Science mean?* or a statement such as *Parental Agency and Family Language Policy.* The capacity to generate usable new content is the product of a process of machine learning. See Banh and Strobel (2023), Lee (2025), Phillips-Wren and Virvou (2025), and Prather et al. (2025) for a comprehensive representation of GenAI.

**Table 2.2:** Key developments in GenAI

| Year | Event | Contribution |
|---|---|---|
| 2014 | Generative Adversarial Networks (GANs) | Deep learning architecture |
| 2017 | Transformers | Neural network architecture |
| 2018 | Bidirectional Encoder Representations from Transformers (BERT) | Machine learning framework for Natural Language Processing |
| 2018 | Generative Pre-trained Transformer (GPT) architecture | Type of Large Language Model |
| 2022 | Launch of ChatGPT | Widely available and efficient Large Language Model |
| 2025 | DeepSeek-R1 | Widely available and efficient Large Language Model |

### 2.2.1 Machine Learning

Machine learning is the process of training machines to carry out tasks independent of human guidance, through a process of deep learning in which complex systems of computer-based neural networks go through training on large sets of data to classify and analyse the data, identifying patterns which can be used to reason, learn and act (Kühl et al., 2022).

Key developments in machine learning have sought to replicate human brain neural network functioning using artificial neural networks. These developments include *Hebbian Learning*, the *Hopfield Network*, the *Boltmann Machine*, *DeepMind*, and *AlphaFold*, as represented in Table 2.3 (Alemanno et al. 2023).

The focus of these developments is the Hebbian principle that "neurons that fire together, wire together" (Alemanno et al. 2023). In a complex AI neural system, this theory proposes that a machine can be trained to memorise and reproduce patterns on the basis that connections between neurons in a neural network become strengthened through repeated and correlated activity. By repeatedly activating a pathway of connections in a machine, the connection pathway becomes stronger and is more likely to be activated and followed with an associated input.

**Table 2.3:** Key developments in machine learning

| Year | Machine Learning Development | Contribution |
|---|---|---|
| 1949 | Hebbian Learning | Donald Hebb conceptualised a model of unsupervised machine learning |
| 1982 | Hopfield Network | John Hopfield developed an AI memory network that could store and recreate patterns based on Hebbian theory |
| 1985 | Boltzman Machine | Geoffrey Hinton and others made advances with their model for unsupervised machine learning |
| 2010 | DeepMind | An AI technology that made machine learning more efficient and with wider applicability |
| 2018 | AlphaFold | Machine learning architecture applied to scientific uses to predict the three-dimensional structures of proteins |

With advances in machine learning, vast datasets are utilised for training to establish these AI neural networks based on repeated and associated patterns. This process can enable a machine to recognise and interpret natural human language with all its characteristics, peculiarities and nuances. Through refining, human-like actions are achieved. See Kühl et al. (2022) for a comprehensive analysis of machine learning.

### 2.2.2 Natural Language Processing

The term Natural Language Processing (NLP) is used to refer to machine learning which specifically is designed to enable computers and machines to understand and communicate with humans (Xu et al., 2024). This could be through handheld devices such as smart phones, tablets, computers or other technology widely used. The training for such processing involves massive numbers of computational linguistic steps which need to be mastered, to facilitate a human-like level of communication. This technology is currently used in chatbots which respond to user or customer commands, prompts and responses. These chatbots can, for example, answer questions without any intervention from a human. They are thus human-like and autonomous. Examples of such chatbots include digital assistants found on smartphones such as Apple's *Siri*, Amazon's *Alexa*, and Microsoft's *Copilot*. This technology also enables the ChatGPT model to be operationalised through GPT-4.5, and the DeepSeek model to be operationalised through DeepSeek-v3. See Xu et al. (2024) for a comprehensive analysis of Natural Language Processing.

### 2.2.3 Large Language Models

While Natural Language Processing focuses on the specific linguistic training components of Artificial Intelligence, Large Language Models (LLM) involve the use of vast volumes of texts as input in the training and development process (Chang et al., 2024). It involves exposing the system to models of human language use to enable identification of patterns, learning and production capacities.

**Table 2.4:** Key developments in large language models

| Year | LLM development | Company |
|---|---|---|
| 2017 | Transformer architecture | Google |
| 2018 | Embeddings from Language Models (ELMo) architecture | Allen Institute for Artificial Intelligence |
| | Generative Pre-trained Transformer (GPT) architecture | OpenAI |
| | Bi-directional Transformer (BERT) architecture | Google |
| 2020 | GPT-3 | OpenAI |
| 2022 | GPT-3.5 | OpenAI |
| 2023 | GPT-4 | OpenAI |
| | DeepSeek coder | DeepSeek |
| 2024 | DeepSeek-v2 | DeepSeek |
| 2025 | DeepSeek-R1 | DeepSeek |

The greater the volume and range of texts used, the better the machine performance. Thus, curated datasets are used in which development teams identify and use source materials they feel will be suitable models of human language use to shape the eventual AI language use created. Key stages in the development and release of Large Language Models (see Wang et al., 2024) are presented in Table 2.4.

We thus use the term Large Language Models (LLM) to describe AI programs that can recognise and generate texts. These LLMs have gone through a process of deep learning to enable the capacity to understand how characters, words, phrases, sentences and paragraphs function together to represent meaning. At the core of the models are parameters which are adjustable values which define the model's behaviour. The most recent LLMs use billions of parameters to achieve set tasks. These parameters are refined with training to perform a wide range of specific tasks.

Two powerful LLMs which have received attention at the time of writing this book are *ChatGPT* and *DeepSeek*. Both these AI models can generate new content. There are distinct differences between the models used by ChatGPT and DeepSeek (Sapkota et al., 2025). We will look at two of these differences.

Firstly, there is a key difference in the way these two models operate. DeepSeek employs what is termed a *Mixture of Experts* (MoE) model, in which only the most relevant components (or parameters as they are technically termed) are activated to respond to specific prompts or tasks. In this approach, a task is subdivided into smaller specialised sub-tasks which are each assigned to 'expert' processing components which have been specifically trained for this approach. The various responses or generated outputs are then re-combined to process the final generated product. ChatGPT, in contrast, employs a *Transformer* model in which information is kept intact and moves in only one direction through layers of processing to generate the task. Both approaches are effective, but reflect different architectural designs used behind the model.

Secondly, DeepSeek is an *open-source* model meaning that it can be modified by a community to suit their needs and preferences. ChatGPT initially started as an open-source model in the development stage but has since transitioned to a *closed-source* model. These two approaches, *open source* and *closed source*, represent different ways of developing and distributing the technology among users and user groups. In open-source models, the code is made available for localised tailoring, whereby, for example, a language group could modify the code to suit local language, culture and value systems, and redistribute the modified form among members of the group. This facility is not so possible in closed-source models, where access to the code is protected and controlled by the developers.

For further reading on LLMs, see AlAfnan (2025), Sapkota et al. (2025) and Xi et al. (2025).

### 2.2.4 Datasets

The datasets used to train LLMs include the following types, in this case relating specifically to ChatGPT (see Liu et al., 2024):

- *CommonCrawl*: over 250 billion pages of open-access text operating across 160 languages
- *Wikipedia*: open-access online encyclopedia with content in over 300 languages

- *WebText*: 8 million documents curated by OpenAI for internal OpenAI use
- Books: electronic versions of published texts representing a wide range of subject areas and languages

Four key features of datasets used for LLM training are: (1) large volumes of raw data in the form of complete texts or text segments; (2) high quality of texts suitable for machine learning designed to replicate or surpass human intelligence and capabilities; (3) range of subject areas to provide for comprehensive and highly specialised comprehension, learning and text generation; (4) range of languages to reflect the linguistic diversity of user groups. For further reading on LLM datasets, see Ostendorff et al. (2024) and Yu et al. (2025).

### 2.2.5 Algorithms

Algorithms are sets of mathematical coded instructions that use parameters to analyse content, learn and create new content. They are designed to enable computers and machines to act intuitively and autonomously (Liu et al., 2023). In the case of Large Language Models (LLM), algorithms attend to central linguistic processes including text summarization, sentiment analysis, and machine translation. Let's explore each of these in turn.

Text summarisation: These algorithms are designed to summarise large volumes of related text to arrive at a text summary which includes all the important information. They do this by identifying and using key sentences or text components within a text.

Sentiment analysis: These algorithms are designed to capture the emotional tone within human language, as positive, neutral or negative, with degrees along this continuum. To exemplify this, LLM learning needs to appreciate the sentiments conveyed in the following statements, not only in attaching a positive or negative rating to the response, but also recognising the degree of positive or negative sentiments conveyed:

- The results exceeded our best expectations.
- If there's a silver lining to the decision, it is the prospects for a fairer funding model in the future.
- The Board shouldn't have been so accommodating of his declared conflict of interest.

Machine translation: These algorithms enable accurate translation of text from one language to another. It does this by matching meanings between two languages.

Algorithms used in Large Language Models (LLM) perform the following linguistic analysis functions (see Ho et al., 2024; Liu et al., 2023):

- Text processing: breaking text into small forms (words, word parts) which can then be used to generate meanings
- Text analysis: analysing tense, parts of speech, phrases
- Semantic analysis: determining text meaning
- Relationship analysis: determining relationships between different parts of text
- Sentiment analysis: determining the emotional tone conveyed within a text
- Text summarisation: reducing a longer text to a summary that retains the core or essential information
- Machine translation: translating from one language to another
- Text-speech processing: converting spoken language to written text and vice versa

For further reading on algorithms used with LLM, see Bandyopadhyay et al. (2025) and van Stein et al. (2025).

## 2.3 GenAI Tools in Higher Education

GenAI tools are typically software applications available on devices such as smart phones, tablets and computers that use AI to both understand and create new content, thereby mimicking the capacity of humans to create. Some of the key areas of development of GenAI (see Aishwarya et al., 2024) are evident in:

- Art generators (e.g., *DALL-E, Midjourney*): These models are capable of generating digital images from prompts in the form of natural language descriptions
- Music generators (e.g., *Hydra II, AIVA, Mubert*): Capable of creating musical pieces
- Video generation (e.g., *AI Studios, Luma Dream Machine, Minimax*): capable of generating video content
- Text generators (e.g., *ChatGPT, Deepseek*): capable of generating text from a prompt

Within universities, GenAI tools have become a key component of learning processes and of writing processes for many university students (Kim et al., 2025). Some of the key documented applications for GenAI in higher education include (see Sousa & Cardoso, 2025):

- Content creation
- Personalised learning
- Coding and computational thinking
- Language learning
- Research and study support
- Presentations and lesson planning
- Assessment and feedback
- STEM education and simulations

An ever-increasing number of GenAI tools are available which can produce structured answers with citations to a prompt (see Hanafi et al., 2025; Jin et al. 2025; McDonald et al., 2025; Wang et al. 2024). Aside from ChatGPT and DeepSeek functionality, GenAI tools available capable of generating cited responses, include:

- Claude
- Consensus
- Elicit
- Jenni
- Litero
- Scite
- Thesis
- Yomu

Studies have suggested some positive experiences with GenAI for various tasks in academic settings from both students and staff, in the form of an assistant with reading, researching, learning, planning and writing (see Belkina et al., 2025). GenAI has been particularly seen as valuable as contributing to a tailored educational experience (Bittle & El-Gayar, 2025). On the other hand, it has been linked to accusations of cheating and breaches of ethical conduct with regard to preparation and presentation of writing for assessment purposes (Belkina et al., 2025).

What is evident is that AI has the capacity to generate coherent responses to some prompts with an academic feel to them (Luo, 2024). For example, studies in subject areas including engineering, medicine and economics have shown the acceptability of GenAI responses (Belkina et al., 2025). Nevertheless, there have been concerns raised about:

- the quality of GenAI responses to more cognitively demanding tasks (see, e.g., Bittle & El-Gayar, 2025)

- possible oversimplification or even misrepresentation of complex research areas by GenAI (Hanafi et al., 2025)
- the capacity of GenAI to appropriately negotiate sensitive or controversial subject areas (Hanafi et al., 2025).

Future iterations of the AI programming are likely to address these concerns.

The availability of GenAI tools in higher education has presented universities with a challenge: how to accommodate GenAI developments and at the same time preserve effective learning systems within degree programs (see Hanafi et al., 2025). The challenge posed by GenAI to valid assessment of student writing within universities has been a particular area of professional and academic interest (see, e.g., Ogunleye et al., 2024).

The cautious response of universities has taken the form of revised and new policies, guidelines and resources for both academics and students (Wang et al., 2024). These tend to operate in two areas:

- Pedagogical applications: designed to promote effective incorporation of GenAI into teaching and learning programs
- Prevention strategies: designed to prevent inappropriate use of GenAI in teaching and learning programs

They also determine the extent of autonomy vested in academics to shape these dual processes of pedagogy and prevention, often with a combination of university-wide policies and guidelines, and authority given to academics to tailor learning and assessment to reflect the complexities posed by GenAI (Wang et al., 2024).

The responses of universities to AI tend to reflect a strong intent within universities to encourage effective and responsible use of GenAI as a learning tool. There is also the underlying fear of improper use of GenAI in academic settings. The underlying thinking in university responses reflects an acceptance of the emerging technology and reflects beliefs about the nature of learning (Luo, 2024). Thus, universities are seeking to balance the realities of the technological advances now available with ethical concerns (Francis et al., 2025). In doing so, students will be given the opportunity to develop responsible and ethical behaviour around use of GenAI which will, it is hoped, continue in their professional lives as AI further develops and becomes intertwined with more components of professional and daily life.

Distinctions are being made between in-class tests which are free of GenAI (i.e., use of GenAI is prohibited) and out of class assignments where use of

GenAI is possible (Luo, 2024). There is also a growing body of work focusing on redesigning assessment tasks to make them AI-proof or limit the scope for use of GenAI (see, e.g., Khlaif et al., 2025).

Some universities have adopted text checking programs developed to identify possible inclusion of GenAI content within a text to discourage students from making unethical use of GenAI content within their writing and identify possible cases for follow-up investigation (Ardito, 2024). These programs started to appear in early 2023 from *Turnitin* and other players including *ZeroGPT, GPTZero, Copyleaks* and *Sapling.* Overall, there is a lack of clarity over whether AI-generated text can be accurately distinguished from human created text, both by humans and by AI detection programs (Luo, 2024), and this remains an area of interest for future research.

While GenAI detection tools are still in relative early development, there is concern about over reliance on them, and the potential for false positives resulting from use of the software, in which student writing free of GenAI is identified by the program as 'likely' to include GenAI content (Ardito, 2024). Some of the key concerns raised regarding the use of such GenAI detecting programs include (see Ardito, 2024):

- Stifling pedagogically-sound use of GenAI: whereby students may be deterred from any experimental use of GenAI in the planning for their writing in the fear that such use may expose them to malpractice accusations
- False positive bias: that false positives may be more associated with some groups than others, with some early evidence of a higher likelihood of false positives for non-native English writers
- Non-verifiable results: that a GenAI detector report cannot be easily verified, leading to possible lengthy and stressful investigations of student writing processes by academic institutions, inducing severe anxiety for affected students

These negative washback effects from the use of GenAI detection programs within higher education on stifling experimental use of the available technology, of false positives, and of stressful follow-up investigations, need to be combatted if universities are to accommodate the developing technology in a positive and pedagogically sound way.

# 3. Vocabulary Profiling

## 3.1 Lexical Nature of Academic Writing

Studies of vocabulary used in academic writing have made distinctions between three groups of words: *high frequency*, *academic* and *technical*. Let's explore each group in turn.

### 3.1.1 High Frequency Words

High frequency words are modelled on West's (1953) *General Service List* (GSL) which was an attempt to capture the most useful 2000 words of the language as a learning goal for English as a Second Language (ESL) students. The list of 2000 high frequency words can be subdivided into the first thousand words (K1) and the second thousand words (K2). The GSL K1 and GSL K2 words are highlighted in the samples of text (see Table 3.1 and Table 3.2).

**Table 3.1:** GSL K1 words in a text

| GSL K1 words |
|---|
| The risk of yellow fever virus (YFV) transmission in the Asia-Pacific region is a growing concern, particularly due to ongoing globalization, international travel, and increasing vector activity. Despite the historical absence of yellow fever in this region, several environmental and ecological factors indicate a potential vulnerability to YFV outbreaks. |

**Table 3.2:** GSL K2 words in a text

| GSL K2 words |
|---|
| The risk of yellow fever virus (YFV) transmission in the Asia-Pacific region is a growing concern, particularly due to ongoing globalization, international travel, and increasing vector activity. Despite the historical absence of yellow fever in this region, several environmental and ecological factors indicate a potential vulnerability to YFV outbreaks. |

These 2000 K1 and K2 words occur frequently in written and spoken language, including, for example, in novels, newspaper stories, academic writing, and EFL coursebooks, representing up to 90 % of the running words (tokens) in some text types (see Table 3.3).

**Table 3.3:** Lexical coverage of K1+K2 words in text types

| Text type | Lexical coverage | Study |
|---|---|---|
| Children's fiction | 90 % | Hirsh & Nation (1992) |
| Newspaper stories | 80 % | Hwang & Nation (1989) |
| Academic texts | 76 % | Coxhead (2000) |
| EFL coursebooks | 90 % | Matsuoka & Hirsh (2010) |

In this regard, they are an essential lexical component in writing.

### 3.1.2 Academic Words

Another group of words in academic writing are academic (or sub-technical) words. These are highlighted in the text sample in Table 3.4.

**Table 3.4:** Academic words in a text

| AWL words |
|---|
| The risk of yellow fever virus (YFV) transmission in the Asia-Pacific region is a growing concern, particularly due to ongoing globalization, international travel, and increasing vector activity. Despite the historical absence of yellow fever in this region, several environmental and ecological factors indicate a potential vulnerability to YFV outbreaks. |

Early attempts to capture the academic (or sub-technical) vocabulary of academic writing include studies conducted in the 1970s.

In the first of these studies, Campion and Elley (1971) constructed an *Academic Vocabulary List* to assist test constructors and examiners in New Zealand with selecting overseas students for admission into university. The word list had two other stated applications: as a guide for selecting words for vocabulary enrichment exercises; and as a tool for estimating the difficulty of prose. Two lists were developed, the *Short List of the 500 Most Common Academic Words* comprising the most essential academic words, and the *Complete Vocabulary List of 3,200 Academic Words* comprising words identified for assessment purposes.

The second of these studies by Praninskas (1972) constructed the *American University Word List* of 507 word families. This list was developed as a basis for instituting a remedial vocabulary course for first year Arabic-speaking students at the American University of Beirut studying in the faculties of arts and sciences.

The completed list provided a principled lexical approach to development of pedagogical materials.

In the third study, Lynn (1973) constructed a list of 197 academic word families to address the identified need for a vocabulary list which reflected the lexical difficulties of Southeast Asian learners of English with reading tasks. The list was used to inform decisions about which words to gloss or highlight in reading texts.

The fourth study by Ghadessy (1979) developed two word lists, a 795-word list and, from this, a select 322-word list to assist in planning the vocabulary development program of first year university students at Pahlavi University in Shiraz, Iran, with acknowledged tailoring for the local educational context.

Building on these four studies, Xue and Nation (1984) developed their *University Word List* (UWL), by finding common ground in the vocabulary lists of Campion and Elley (1971), Praninskas (1972), Lynn (1973) and Ghadessy (1979). The UWL used frequency and range criteria to identify 737 academic word families beyond the first 2000 words of English. This list provided 8.5 % lexical coverage of a broad range of academic texts.

More recently, Coxhead (2000) adopted a fresh approach to identifying academic vocabulary in the form of her *Academic Word List* (AWL). She constructed an academic corpus representative of the texts first year undergraduate students are likely to meet at university, covering 28 subject areas across arts, commerce, law and science, as follows:

- Arts
  - Education
  - History
  - Linguistics
  - Philosophy
  - Politics
  - Psychology
  - Sociology

- Commerce
  - Accounting
  - Economics
  - Finance
  - Industrial Relations
  - Management
  - Marketing
  - Public Policy

- Law
  - Constitutional Law
  - Criminal Law
  - Family Law and Medico-Legal
  - International Law
  - Pure Commercial Law
  - Quasi-Commercial Law
  - Rights and Remedies

- Science
  - Biology
  - Chemistry
  - Computer Science
  - Geography
  - Geology
  - Mathematics
  - Physics

In her study, Coxhead excluded high frequency words, and considered word frequency, range and uniformity across the corpus to identify 570 academic words providing between 8 % and 12 % lexical coverage of a range of academic texts.

### 3.1.3 Technical Words

Another group of words appearing in academic texts is technical words. These are highlighted in the text sample in Table 3.5.

**Table 3.5:** Technical words in a text

| Technical words |
|---|
| The risk of yellow fever virus (YFV) transmission in the Asia-Pacific region is a growing concern, particularly due to ongoing globalization, international travel, and increasing vector activity. Despite the historical absence of yellow fever in this region, several environmental and ecological factors indicate a potential vulnerability to YFV outbreaks. |

These words are much more commonly used in one discipline or subject area than in other subject areas across a university.

**Table 3.6:** Science words

| **Sample of science words (Coxhead & Hirsh, 2007)** | | |
|---|---|---|
| absorb | flora | photosynthesis |
| acid | fluid | pigment |
| acute | fungus | pore |
| alcohol | fuel | protein |
| algae | gravity | saturate |
| ancestor | humid | species |
| atmosphere | hydrogen | symmetry |
| bacteria | intestine | synthetic |
| carbohydrate | magnesium | temperate |
| carbon | marine | thermal |
| climate | microscope | toxic |
| decompose | moisture | vacuum |
| digest | nitrogen | wavelength |
| electrode | orbit | |
| enzyme | | |

In this regard, they are subject-dependent. To illustrate this, the words in Table 3.6 assume a technical function in science. Within science, more specialised technical lists have been identified to reflect the vocabulary of biology, chemistry and physics, as represented in Table 3.7 (Matsuoka & Hirsh, 2018)

**Table 3.7:** Biology, chemistry and physics words

| **Biology** | **Chemistry** | **Physics** |
|---|---|---|
| amino | ammonia | battery |
| cellular | carbonate | capacitor |
| chromosome | catalyst | friction |
| ecosystem | combustion | generator |
| gene | corrode | helium |
| hormone | dilute | hertz |
| immune | dissolve | induction |
| inherit | electrolysis | momentum |
| mammal | ethanol | quantum |
| nutrient | hydrocarbon | refractive |
| organic | hydroxide | relativity |
| parasite | organic | stationary |
| respiration | oxidation | torque |
| seed | precipitate | ultrasound |
| soil | soluble | vector |
| species | solvent | velocity |
| virus | sulphur | volt |

Collectively, K1, K2, AWL and technical words account for most of the words appearing in an academic text.

### 3.1.4 Proper Nouns

Additional words appearing in academic writing include proper nouns (e.g., names of people, places, organisations). Proper nouns are shown in Table 3.8, in this case identifying a regional area.

**Table 3.8:** Proper nouns appearing in a text

| Proper nouns |
|---|
| The risk of yellow fever virus (YFV) transmission in the Asia-Pacific region is a growing concern, particularly due to ongoing globalization, international travel, and increasing vector activity. Despite the historical absence of yellow fever in this region, several environmental and ecological factors indicate a potential vulnerability to YFV outbreaks. |

There is no particular vocabulary learning burden attached to proper nouns as the meaning is often clear from context.

### 3.1.5 Low Frequency Words

Low frequency words include a vast number of lexical items. By definition, they occur comparatively rarely in the language, and, when used, will often appear only once or twice in a text. Low frequency words which may appear in some academic texts include the following:

*ubiquitous, maleficence, obfuscate, commensurate, trepidation*

If low frequency words appear frequently in one subject area, this may reflect a technical role of the word.

## 3.2 K1, K2 and AWL Word Lists

Three word lists capture much of the vocabulary appearing in academic writing: the first thousand-word list based on West's (1953) GSL (termed *GSL K1*), the second thousand-word list based on West's (1953) GSL (termed *GSL K2*), and Coxhead's (2000) Academic Word List (termed *AWL*). These three word lists, grouping words into word families, are referred to in the current book as:

- GSL K1 (or K1)
- GSL K2 (or K2)
- AWL

A sample of words from each word list is presented in Table 3.9.

**Table 3.9:** GSL K1, GSL K2 and AWL words

| |
|---|
| GSL K1<br>the, of, in, age, because, child, country, dream, employ, factory, gentle, have, increase, length, many, mother, nature, observe, party, people, recognise, science, table, understand, voice, winter |
| GSL K2<br>ambition, astonish, awkward, birth, calculate, curious, decrease, educate, forgive, guest, harvest, instrument, journey, liberty, medicine, nephew, overcome, persuade, quantity, reputation, salary, weigh |
| AWL<br>abandon, benefit, constrain, derive, ensure, federal, generate, guarantee, hierarchy, innovate, locate, mechanism, modify, precede, random, suspend, tradition, utilise, vehicle, voluntary, widespread |

There is no single technical word list for academic settings, given that each discipline and subject area has its distinctive subject-specific collection of technical words. Thus, we tend to use the term *other words* for those appearing in a text and not appearing in the GSL K1, GSL K2 and AWL lists.

**Table 3.10:** Lexical profile of four academic texts

| Text | Length (tokens) | Lexical coverage (%) | | | |
|---|---|---|---|---|---|
| | | K1 | K2 | AWL | Other words |
| Arts text | 8752 | 68.5 | 5.7 | 11.3 | 14.5 |
| Econ text | 3386 | 70.4 | 4.5 | 10.3 | 14.7 |
| Law text | 12726 | 80.8 | 4.5 | 6.4 | 8.3 |
| Sci text | 2305 | 70.0 | 5.2 | 9.7 | 15.1 |

Hirsh (2010) carried out a vocabulary profile analysis of word use in four research articles appearing in journals covering arts, economics, law and science, with reporting of lexical coverage for the K1, K2, AWL and *other words* (see Table 3.10).

These four texts show variability in word length, and, more importantly for the current study, in use of vocabulary. The use of GSL K1 words varies quite markedly between 68.5 % and 80.8 %. Use of GSL K2 words is between 4.5 % and 5.7 %. Use of AWL words varies between 6.4 % and 11.3 %, while use of *other words* including many technical words ranges from 8.3 % to 15.1 %. Overall, the data reflect expected variance in vocabulary use to reflect the technicality of writing, individual styles of writers, and the components within the research articles. The law text stands out as making greater use of K1 words and less use of AWL and *other words*, with minimal observable impact on use of K2 words.

## 3.3 BNC-COCA Word Lists

Developments in computing over the past decades have permitted the assembly of very large corpora (electronic collections) of texts for various research or educational purposes.

One of these is the *British National Corpus* (BNC) with over 100 million words (Leech & Rayson, 2014). The collection includes representative samples of both written and spoken language from a wide range of sources. The written component represents 90 % of the corpus covering regional and national newspapers, specialist periodicals and journals, academic books, popular fiction, letters and memoranda, school and university essays. The spoken part representing 10 % of the corpus includes transcribed conversations from informal and formal settings including business settings, government meetings, and radio shows.

Another very large corpus is the *Corpus of Contemporary American English* (COCA) with over 1 billion words (Davies, 2009). This corpus also has both written and spoken components covering: fiction, popular magazines, newspapers, academic texts, television programs, movie subtitles, blogs, and other web pages.

Paul Nation has developed word lists at word divisions from K1 to K20 and beyond for the combined BNC-COCA corpora to provide a comprehensive representation of the vocabulary of modern English.

**Table 3.11:** Levels of word families

| |
|---|
| Level 1<br>A different form is a different word. Capitalization is ignored. |
| Level 2<br>Regularly inflected words are part of the same family. The inflectional categories are - plural; third person singular present tense; past tense; past participle; -ing; comparative; superlative; possessive. |
| Level 3<br>-able, -er, -ish, -less, -ly, -ness, -th, -y, non-, un-, all with restricted uses. |

| |
|---|
| Level 4<br>-al, -ation, -ess, -ful, -ism, -ist, -ity, -ize, -ment, -ous, in-, all with restricted uses. |
| Level 5<br>-age (leakage), -al (arrival), -ally (idiotically), -an (American), -ance (clearance), -ant (consultant), -ary (revolutionary), -atory (confirmatory), -dom (kingdom; officialdom), -eer (black marketeer), -en (wooden), -en (widen), -ence (emergence), -ent (absorbent), -ery (bakery; trickery), -ese (Japanese; officialese), -esque (picturesque), -ette (usherette; roomette), -hood (childhood), -i (Israeli), -ian (phonetician; Johnsonian), -ite (Paisleyite; also chemical meaning), -let (coverlet), -ling (duckling), -ly (leisurely), -most (topmost), -ory (contradictory), -ship (studentship), -ward (homeward), -ways (crossways), -wise (endwise; discussion-wise), anti- (anti-inflation), ante- (anteroom), arch- (archbishop), bi- (biplane), circum- (circumnavigate), counter- (counter-attack), en- (encage; enslave), ex- (expresident), fore- (forename), hyper- (hyperactive), inter- (inter-African, interweave), mid- (mid-week), mis- (misfit), neo- (neo-colonialism), post- (post-date), pro- (pro-British), semi- (semi-automatic), sub- (subclassify; subterranean), un- (untie; unburden). |
| Level 6<br>-able, -ee, -ic, -ify, -ion, -ist, -ition, -ive, -th, -y, pre-, re-. |

The principle applied to construct the BNC-COCA word lists is grouping words into word families. This grouping was based on Bauer and Nation's (1993) *Levels of Affixation*, whereby words are included in the word family if they meet the description of affixes shown in Level 2 to Level 6 (see Table 3.11).

The resulting BNC-COCA K1 to K20 lists contain approximately one thousand headwords each, but many thousand word types if we include all family members. Table 3.12 provides a picture of these word lists in terms of the occurrence of ecological terms across the lists.

**Table 3.12:** Occurrence of ecology words in BNC-COCA word lists

| Word list | Words appearing at this BNC-COCA frequency level |
|---|---|
| K1 | bear, cat, dog, rabbit |
| K2 | elephant, fox, lion, mouse |
| K3 | migrate, ocean, remote, silk, territory |
| K4 | dolphin, eagle, fox, lion, mouse, owl |
| K5 | ant, spider |
| K6 | beetle, camel, crow, chimpanzee, falcon, hare, parrot |
| K7 | buffalo, ferret |
| K8 | beaver, gorilla, leopard, otter, vulture |
| K9 | coyote, kangaroo, moose, sparrow, zebra |
| K10 | baboon, cheetah, giraffe, hedgehog, locust |
| K11 | caribou, grasshopper, porpoise, rhinoceros, skunk, sloth |
| K12 | gazelle, llama, orangutang, porcupine, racoon, walrus |

*(Continued)*

**Table 3.12:** *(Continued)*

| Word list | Words appearing at this BNC-COCA frequency level |
|---|---|
| K13 | cougar, mongoose, wildebeest |
| K14 | chipmunk, lemur |
| K15 | manatee, mayfly, wombat |
| K16 | platypus, warthog |
| K17 | |
| K18 | aardvark, skink |
| K19 | |
| K20 | |

One interesting consideration is that, for these lists based principally around descending frequency of occurrence as we progress from K1 to K20, there will be some well-known words appearing low on the list reflecting their relatively low occurrence in the BNC-COCA combined corpora. Examples include *giraffe* (K10), *rhinoceros* (K11) and *porcupine* (K12). This reflects a characteristic of language where objects of interest, such as wild animals or those located in zoos, can be widely known yet relatively rarely appearing in written (and spoken) texts.

Another characteristic of the language is that subject-specific technical words associated with a single subject area can appear anywhere in the lists from K1 through to K20 and beyond. This is because the highly specialised role of a word in a single subject area can differ from its pattern of behaviour in the general language.

As a rule though, the lower words appear on the K1 to K20 lists, the less likely they are to be met in the general language.

# 4. The Current Study

The focus of the current study is the lexical profile of AI-generated texts representing academic topic areas. GenAI in this context refers to tools based on computer algorithms capable of creating and understanding digital content. An increasing number of GenAI tools are available which can produce structured answers with citations to a prompt (see Hanafi et al., 2025). GenAI tools used by students and academics in higher education to generate academic texts include:

- Claude
- Consensus
- Elicit
- Jenni
- Litero
- Scite
- Thesis
- Yomu

With these GenAI tools, a response text can be generated based on a prompt. Tools are increasingly allowing degrees of tailoring, including use of keywords, pre-selection of citation texts, scope of analysis, length of response generated, and checking of partial responses giving the user the option to generate a response that serves their needs or requirements.

## 4.1 Selection of GenAI Tools

Three GenAI tools were selected in the current study for the purposes of generating AI content from specific prompts. The three GenAI tools were selected based on:

- Suitability for specialised academic subject area responses
- Creation of quite comprehensive responses
- Answers with links to reference materials (either visible or hidden in the generated text)
- Responses of roughly similar word length

The three GenAI tools selected were:

- Scite: selected to display citations
- Jenni: selected to display citations
- Yomu: selected to hide citations

The three GenAI tools were selected due to their availability and functionality in producing academic texts from a prompt with clear sourcing to the available literature (see Table 4.1).

**Table 4.1:** Selection of GenAI tools

| GenAI tool | Tool functionability |
|---|---|
| Scite AI | Generates text with citations appearing in the text to published research. Trained to query its citation index and provide answers based on genuine research data. This is in response to a prompt. |
| Jenni AI | Generates text with citations appearing in the text to published research. It is specifically tailored for writing and research assistance. It operates in response to a prompt. |
| Yomu AI | Generates text with the option to hide or show citations to published research. It is designed to help academics and students write research papers as well as other types of texts. This is in response to a prompt. |

The following displays the introductory section of GenAI texts for each GenAI tool in response to a science-related prompt on the topic *Risk of Yellow Fever Virus Transmission in the Asia-Pacific Region*.

Science: Scite AI

> The risk of yellow fever virus (YFV) transmission in the Asia-Pacific region is a growing concern, particularly due to ongoing globalization, international travel, and increasing vector activity. Despite the historical absence of yellow fever in this region, several environmental and ecological factors indicate a potential vulnerability to YFV outbreaks.

The Aedes aegypti mosquito, which is an efficient vector for YFV, has established itself in many tropical and subtropical regions, including parts of Asia. The presence of Aedes spp. does not directly correlate with the transmission of yellow fever; however, the density of these mosquito populations in urban areas poses a concerning risk factor. Urbanization often leads to increased human-mosquito interaction, creating opportunities for viral transmission if the virus were introduced through travel (Shearer et al., 2018; Shinde et al., 2024). Countries like China, which have documented imported cases of YFV, demonstrate the potential for local transmission if epidemiological conditions align (Kuno, 2020; Zhao et al., 2018).

## Science: Jenni AI

The Asia-Pacific region, encompassing a vast archipelago of diverse ecosystems and densely populated urban centers, faces a significant yet often overlooked threat from yellow fever virus. While yellow fever is not currently endemic in the region, the potential for its introduction and subsequent transmission is a growing concern due to several converging factors (Ortiz-Martínez et al., 2017). Increased global travel and trade, coupled with the presence of competent mosquito vectors such as Aedes aegypti and Aedes albopictus, create pathways for the virus to enter and establish itself in new areas (Ramachari & Purushothaman, 2019). The ecological and epidemiological landscape of the Asia-Pacific region shares similarities with areas in Africa and the Americas where yellow fever is endemic, heightening the risk of its emergence (Espinal et al., 2019). Understanding the interplay of vector biology, environmental drivers, and human behavior is crucial for assessing the risk of yellow fever virus transmission in the Asia-Pacific region and implementing effective preventive measures (Abdullahi et al., 2021). The absence of widespread immunity to yellow fever in the human population of the Asia-Pacific region further exacerbates the potential for large-scale outbreaks if the virus is introduced (Irsal et al., 2023; Nakase et al., 2024).

## Science: Yomu AI

Yellow fever is a viral infection transmitted by mosquitoes, primarily affecting humans and nonhuman primates. It is endemic to parts of Africa and South America and is caused by a virus belonging to the Flavivirus genus. This disease is characterized by a sudden onset of fever, chills, muscle pain, headache, nausea, and fatigue. In severe cases, it can lead to jaundice, bleeding, and potentially fatal kidney and liver impairment.

Historically, the Asia-Pacific region, encompassing countries such as China, India, Japan, Indonesia, and others, remains free of yellow fever despite the prevalence of suitable environmental conditions and vectors like Aedes mosquitoes, which theoretically could support the virus. The absence of the virus in this heavily populated area raises questions regarding future risks, especially in the context of increased global travel and changing climate patterns.

As displayed, the texts generated by Scite and Jenni include visible citations, while the text generated by Yomu has citations hidden from view. There is an option to display these.

## 4.2 Selection of Prompts for GenAI Text Generation

The current study utilises four prompts representing the title of four published non-GenAI research papers representing arts, commerce, law and science, as follows:

- *Bourdieu, Social Capital and Online Interaction* - representing arts
- *Paid Parental Leave and Children's Schooling Outcomes* - representing commerce
- *Anti-Social Behaviour, Behavioural Expectations and an Urban Aesthetic* - representing law
- *Risk of Yellow Fever Virus Transmission in the Asia-Pacific Region* - representing science

For each non-GenAI text, three corresponding GenAI texts are prepared, giving rise to 16 texts in total, as follows (with total word count provided in brackets):

Arts: Bourdieu, Social Capital and Online Interaction

- non-GenAI (7002)
- Scite (962)
- Jenni (827)
- Yomu (963)

Commerce: Paid Parental Leave and Children's Schooling Outcomes

- non-GenAI (4426)
- Scite (881)
- Jenni (1075)
- Yomu (1003)

Law: Anti-Social Behaviour, Behavioural Expectations and an Urban Aesthetic

- non-GenAI (5782)
- Scite (962)
- Jenni (1185)
- Yomu (870)

Science: Risk of Yellow Fever Virus Transmission in the Asia-Pacific Region

- non-GenAI (3405)
- Scite (736)
- Jenni (798)
- Yomu (891)

In each case, the non-GenAI text is substantially longer than the three GenAI texts. This reflects the role of the non-GenAI texts in presenting new insights through inclusion of study methods and results. The three GenAI texts are of more comparable word lengths. In each case, the complete available text word length is indicated here (excluding references and appendices in the case of the non-GenAI texts).

## 4.3 Analysis of Texts

The 16 resulting texts were firstly run through the following lexical profiling program available at Cobb's (2025) *Compleat Lexical Tutor* website:

- Web VP Classic: utilising the GSL K1, GSL K2 and AWL word lists

This was to provide a lexical profile of GSL K1, GSL K2, AWL and *other words* for each text, with the primary interest being the lexical coverage of each.

Web VP Classic Output

| | Families | Types | Tokens | Percent |
|---|---|---|---|---|
| **K1 Words (1-1000):** | 399 | 627 | **4985** | **71.19%** |
| Function: | ... | ... | (3026) | (43.22%) |
| Content: | ... | ... | (1959) | (27.98%) |
| > Anglo-Sax | ... | ... | (664) | (9.48%) |
| **K2 Words (1001-2000):** | 72 | 90 | **181** | **2.58%** |
| > Anglo-Sax | ... | ... | (48) | (0.69%) |
| 1k+2k | | | ... | (73.77%) |
| **AWL Words:** | 203 | 336 | **866** | **12.37%** |
| > Anglo-Sax | ... | ... | (41) | (0.59%) |
| **Off-List Words:** | ? | 310 | 970 | 13.85% |
| | 674+? | 1363 | 7002 | 100% |

| **Current profile** | |
|---|---|
| **%** | **Cumul.** |
| 71.19 | 71.19 |
| 2.58 | 73.77 |
| **12.37** | 86.14 |
| 13.85 | 100.00 |

| | |
|---|---|
| Words in text (tokens): | 7002 |
| Different words (types): | 1363 |
| Type-token ratio: | 0.19 |
| Tokens per type: | 5.14 |
| Lex density (content words/total) | 0.57 |
| *Pertaining to onlist only* | |
| Tokens: | 6032 |
| Types: | 1053 |
| Families: | 674 |
| Tokens per family: | 8.95 |
| Types per family: | 1.56 |
| Anglo-Sax Index: (A-Sax tokens + functors / onlist tokens) | % |
| Greco-Lat/Fr-Cognate Index: (Inverse of above) | % |

**Figure 4.1:** Sample output for VocabProfile.

An example of the resulting output files is displayed in Figure 4.1. The output file was utilised to collect raw data which are presented as a summary in Table 4.2.

**Table 4.2:** Sample data from VocabProfile

| | Families | Types | Tokens | Percent (%) | Cumulative % |
|---|---|---|---|---|---|
| **K1** | 399 | 627 | 4985 | 71.19 | 71.19 |
| **K2** | 72 | 90 | 181 | 2.58 | 73.77 |
| **AWL** | 203 | 336 | 866 | 12.37 | 86.14 |
| **Other words** | - | 310 | 970 | 13.85 | 100.00 |

To appreciate the data presented in Table 4.2, the following key is provided explaining use of key terminology.

Key:

| | |
|---|---|
| Families | counts the total number of different word families from each word list appearing in the text (regardless of number of times each word family occurs). Thus, 399 indicates that 399 of 1000 K1 families were used in this text. |
| Types | counts the total number of different word types from each word list appearing in the text (regardless of number of times each word type occurs). Some types will be from the same word family. |
| Tokens | counts the total number of individual word occurrences (also termed running words) in the text from each word list. Thus, 4985 for K1 indicates that K1 words occur 4985 times in the text. |
| Percent | presents the percentage of tokens in the text from each word list. Thus, 71.19 % for K1 indicates that K1 words account for 71.19 % of all tokens in the text. |
| Cumulative | progressively adds lexical coverage for each word list or *other words* to attain 100 % total. |

While word families are counted for K1, K2 and AWL lists based on prepared word lists, word family counts are not provided for *other words* due to unavailability of valid word family lists based on this division of words.

The text coverage data for GSL K1, GSL K2, AWL and *other words* for four texts in each subject area (arts, commerce, law, science) were then summarised in a table and a figure for visual comparison, as shown in Table 4.3 and Figure 4.2.

**Table 4.3:** Sample summary data from VocabProfile

| | Text coverage of tokens (%) | | | |
|---|---|---|---|---|
| **(Arts)** | **Non-GenAI** | **GenAI: Scite** | **GenAI: Jenni** | **GenAI: Yomu** |
| **K1** | 71.19 | 57.28 | 59.73 | 59.09 |
| **K2** | 2.58 | 4.89 | 3.26 | 3.01 |
| **AWL** | 12.37 | 20.27 | 19.95 | 23.47 |
| **Other words** | 13.85 | 17.57 | 17.05 | 14.43 |

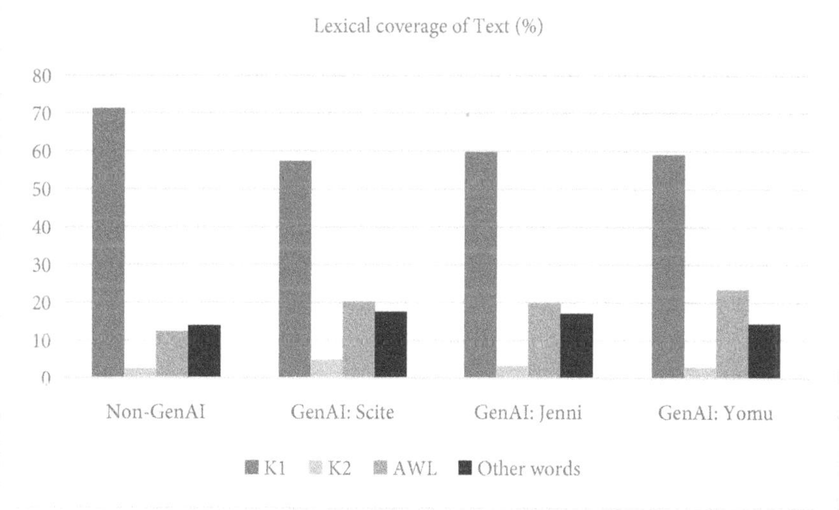


**Figure 4.2:** Sample summary data from VocabProfile.

The 16 resulting texts were next run through the following lexical profiling program available at Cobb's (2025) *Compleat Lexical Tutor* website:

- Compleat Web VP: utilising BNC-COCA K1 to K20 word lists

| Freq. Level | Families (%) | Types (%) | Tokens (%) | Cumul. token (%) |
|---|---|---|---|---|
| K-1 : | 115 (42.1) | 131 (40.43) | 464 (54.653) | 54.7 |
| K-2 : | 49 (17.9) | 63 (19.44) | 177 (20.848) | 75.5 |
| K-3 : | 69 (25.3) | 84 (25.93) | 136 (16.019) | 91.5 |
| K-4 : | 21 (7.7) | 22 (6.79) | 33 (3.887) | 95.4 |
| K-5 : | 6 (2.2) | 7 (2.16) | 13 (1.531) | 96.9 |
| K-6 : | 1 (0.4) | 1 (0.31) | 1 (0.118) | 97.1 |
| K-7 : | 3 (1.1) | 3 (0.93) | 3 (0.353) | 97.4 |
| K-8 : | 3 (1.1) | 3 (0.93) | 4 (0.471) | 97.9 |
| K-9 : | 2 (0.7) | 2 (0.62) | 2 (0.236) | 98.1 |
| K-10 : | | | | - |
| K-11 : | 2 (0.7) | 2 (0.62) | 2 (0.236) | 98.4 |
| K-12 : | | | | - |
| K-13 : | 1 (0.4) | 1 (0.31) | 1 (0.118) | 98.5 |
| K-14 : | 1 (0.4) | 1 (0.31) | 4 (0.471) | 98.9 |
| K-15 : | | | | - |
| K-16 : | | | | - |
| K-17 : | | | | - |
| K-18 : | | | | - |
| K-19 : | | | | - |
| K-20 : | | | | - |

**Figure 4.3:** Sample K1-K10 raw data.

This was to generate data on the lexical coverage as percentage (%) for the BNC-COCA K1 to K10 word lists, to provide a lexical analysis based on word frequency. These word lists group words into word families. An example of the resulting output files is displayed in Figure 4.3.

From this output, a table was generated to display the respective lexical frequency as percentage (%) for each BNC-COCA K1 to K10 word list, as illustrated in Table 4.4.

**Table 4.4:** Sample K1-K10 data

| | non-GenAI | Gen-AI Scite | GenAI Jenni | GenAI Yomu |
|---|---|---|---|---|
| K1 | 69.48 | 54.25 | 54.65 | 51.07 |
| K2 | 13.88 | 22.12 | 20.85 | 23.75 |
| K3 | 10.77 | 16.22 | 16.02 | 18.86 |
| K4 | 1.83 | 3.40 | 3.89 | 2.75 |
| K5 | 0.40 | 1.20 | 1.53 | 1.53 |
| K6 | 0.24 | 0.50 | 0.12 | 1.22 |
| K7 | 0.37 | 0.30 | 0.35 | 0.31 |
| K8 | 0.25 | 0.60 | 0.47 | 0.10 |
| K9 | 0.14 | 0.10 | 0.24 | 0 |
| K10 | 0.13 | 0 | 0 | 0.10 |

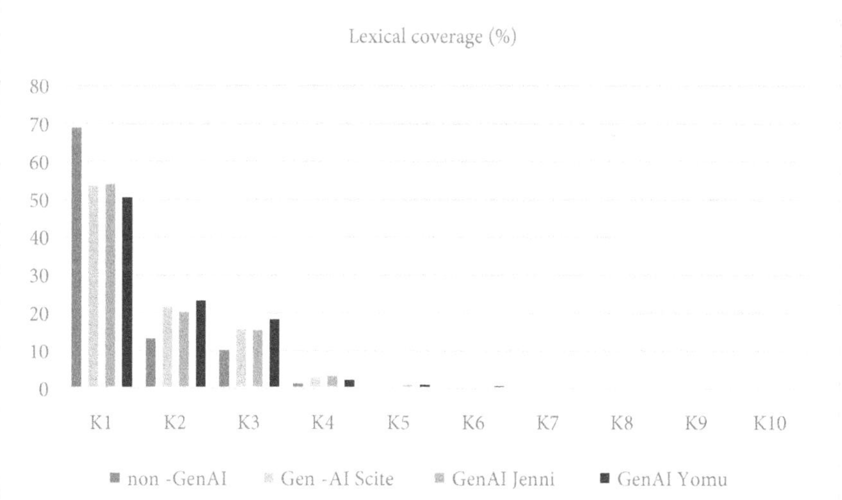


**Figure 4.4:** Sample K1-K10 data.

The data are then displayed in a figure for easier visual comparison across each group of four texts, with separate reporting for arts, commerce, law and science. An example is shown in Figure 4.4

As a third stage in the analysis, the 16 texts were run through a word family frequency profiler using the following lexical profiling program available at Cobb's (2025) *Compleat Lexical Tutor* website:

- The Compleat Word Lister: presents content word families appearing in descending order of frequency (whereby function words are excluded from the reporting)

This was to provide a raw data list for each text of the 20 most frequently occurring content words, with total number of occurrences for each text provided. An example of the resulting output files for content words is displayed in Figure 4.5.

<u>FAMILIES COUNT</u>

Tokens : 835 - Families: 277
Function words excluded
FAMS
BY FREQ

36_social
28_capital
20_number
20_online
14_digital
14_individuals
8_&
8_cultural
7_bourdieu
7_interactions
6_field
5_al
5_et
5_networks
5_resources
5_understanding
4_access
4_concepts
4_connections
4_dynamics
4_economic
4_fields
4_habitus

**Figure 4.5:** Content words data.

In this list, the term 'number' appearing third from the top relates to any numeric numbers, dates and statistics (e.g., 1, 10 %, 2025) appearing in the text. This lexical item was excluded from the analysis and reporting. Also excluded are any function words appearing, as the program does permit some function words to appear. Also, as counting is designed to be as word families, there is a need to combine separate listings for members of the same word family in some cases when they appear. The subsequent list displays the 20 most frequently occurring content words in each text in descending order. This is presented in a table, as illustrated in Table 4.5.

**Table 4.5:** Sample content words data

| Non-GenAI | GenAI Scite | GenAI Jenni | GenAI Yomu |
|---|---|---|---|
| social | social | social | social |
| capital | capital | capital | capital |
| Bourdieu | online | online | online |
| online | interactions | digital | Bourdieu |
| digital | individuals | individuals | cultural |
| interactions | connections | field | networks |
| internet | digital | Bourdieu | digital |
| individuals | Bourdieu | cultural | interactions |
| memes | networks | interactions | individuals |
| habitus | relationships | networks | platforms |
| American | platforms | resources | access |
| field | bridging | understanding | media |
| meme | communication | access | traditional |
| knowledge | ties | concepts | challenges |
| distinction | bonding | connections | network |
| good | communities | dynamics | relationships |
| group | lee | economic | concept |
| information | offline | habitus | implications |
| inhabitants | resources | outcomes | interaction |
| new | studies | platforms | leverage |

For the final stage of analysis, the 16 texts were run through the following lexical profiling program available at Cobb's (2025) *Compleat Lexical Tutor* website:

- Compleat Web VP: utilising BNC-COCA K1 to K20 word lists

This was to identify word occurrence (as word families) from the BNC-COCA K5 to K20 word lists, to provide a lexical analysis of words occurring which assume an overall lower frequency in the general language. It is assumed that some of these word occurrences will be assuming a technical (or subject-specific) role in the text in which they appear.

In order to generate approximately equal numbers of lexical items between the non-GenAI text and the three GenAI texts, the non-GenAI text length was adjusted. Complete middle sections of the texts were used in this case. The resulting word counts across the four texts for arts, commerce, law and science are displayed.

| Arts | Word length (tokens) |
|---|---|
| non-GenAI | 1262 |
| Gen-AI: Scite | 962 |
| Gen-AI: Jenni | 827 |
| Gen-AI: Yomu | 963 |

| Commerce | Word length (tokens) |
|---|---|
| non-GenAI | 2843 |
| Gen-AI: Scite | 881 |
| Gen-AI: Jenni | 1075 |
| Gen-AI: Yomu | 1003 |

| Law | Word length (tokens) |
|---|---|
| non-GenAI | 2363 |
| Gen-AI: Scite | 962 |
| Gen-AI: Jenni | 1185 |
| Gen-AI: Yomu | 870 |

| Science | Word length (tokens) |
|---|---|
| non-GenAI | 822 |
| Gen-AI: Scite | 736 |
| Gen-AI: Jenni | 798 |
| Gen-AI: Yomu | 891 |

The resulting raw data of word family occurrences for BNC-COCA K5 to K20 word lists are displayed in a table for each group of 4 texts, with individual reporting for arts, commerce, law, and science, as in Table 4.6.

**Table 4.6:** Sample low frequency words data

| | non-GenAI | GenAI: Scite | GenAI: Jenni | GenAI: Yomu |
|---|---|---|---|---|
| K5-K20 | appropriated | bolster | agonist | advent |
| | conjunction | buffer | dialect | algorithm |
| | deplore | conversely | disposition | amplify |
| | dialectic | drawback | dynamics | appropriated |
| | dichotomy | dynamics | encompass | devalue |
| | disinterested | encompass | foundationalism | dilute |
| | disposition | equate | habitus | disparity |
| | engender | excursion | ingrain | disseminate |
| | formative | expanse | interplay | durable |
| | habitus | extrovert | reap | dynamics |
| | hypocrite | habitus | reciprocity | egalitarian |
| | incite | interplay | socialise | embed |
| | italic | intersect | strata | entrench |
| | lingo | necessitate | stratify | erosion |
| | meme | nuance | tan | foundationalism |
| | microcosm | pandemic | tangible | intellect |
| | mitre | pivot | underscore | Interplay |
| | mitt | posit | upbringing | necessitate |
| | pertinent | proactive | | perpetuate |
| | proficient | robust | | reshape |
| | sunder | theorise | | transient |
| | typeset | transactional | | twine |
| | volition | transcend | | ubiquitous |
| | wherein | underscore | | |

Table 4.6 thus provides a profile of low frequency words for each text, including many words expected to be assuming a technical function, listed alphabetically by combining all the listings as a single K5 to K20 group.

# 5. Analysis 1: K1, K2 and AWL Words

This chapter presents a lexical analysis of the non-GenAI text and the three GenAI texts, with separate reporting for arts, commerce, law and science. The analysis displays the lexical coverage as percentage (%) for the following groups of words:

- GSL K1 (first thousand-word list as word families)
- GSL K2 (second thousand-word list as word families)
- AWL (academic word list of 570 word families)
- *other words* (including technical words, proper nouns and low frequency words, presented as word types)

The following key is provided for interpretation of data.

Key:

| | |
|---|---|
| Families | counts the total number of different word families from each word list appearing in the text (regardless of number of times each word family occurs). Thus, 399 indicates that 399 of 1000 K1 families were used in this text. |
| Types | counts the total number of different word types from each word list appearing in the text (regardless of number of times each word type occurs). Some types will be from the same word family. |
| Tokens | counts the total number of individual word occurrences (also termed running words) in the text from each word list. Thus, 4985 for K1 indicates that K1 words occur 4985 times in the text. |
| Percent | presents the percentage of tokens in the text from each word list. Thus, 71.19 % for K1 indicates that K1 words account for 71.19 % of all tokens in the text. |
| Cumulative | progressively adds lexical coverage for each word list or *other words* to attain 100 % total. |

## 5.1 Arts Texts

The following analysis is for the four arts texts.

### 5.1.1 Non-GenAI

The non-GenAI arts text is a research article titled *Bourdieu, Social Capital and Online Interaction* published in *Sociology* in 2015. This text was analysed with VocabProfile with the following result output (see Table 5.1).

**Table 5.1:** VocabProfile of arts non-GenAI text

| | Families | Types | Tokens | Percent (%) | Cumulative % |
|---|---|---|---|---|---|
| K1 | 399 | 627 | 4985 | 71.19 | 71.19 |
| K2 | 72 | 90 | 181 | 2.58 | 73.77 |
| AWL | 203 | 336 | 866 | 12.37 | 86.14 |
| Other words | - | 310 | 970 | 13.85 | 100.00 |
| Words in text (tokens): 7002 | | | | | |

Table 5.1 indicates the percentage of tokens (running words) in the text from each of the word lists (K1, K2, AWL) and *other words* (which covers technical words, numbers, proper nouns and/or low frequency words). For this text, the first thousand-word list (K1) represents 71.19 % of tokens, while the second thousand words (K2) contributes a further 2.58 %. Collectively, the first two thousand words represent 73.77 % of tokens. Beyond this use of high frequency words, the text makes use of academic words (AWL) representing 12.37 % of tokens. Remaining word use in the text categorised as *other words* is likely to include substantial use of technical words covering 13.85 % of tokens.

These data on lexical coverage (percent) of the K1, K2, AWL and *other words* in this text are reviewed in Section 5.1.5. as a summary of the four arts texts.

### 5.1.2 GenAI Scite

The Scite AI arts text was generated from the prompt "Bourdieu, Social Capital and Online Interaction". This text was analysed with VocabProfile with the following result output (see Table 5.2).

**Table 5.2:** VocabProfile of arts GenAI: Scite text

| | Families | Types | Tokens | Percent (%) | Cumulative % |
|---|---|---|---|---|---|
| K1 | 131 | 157 | 551 | 57.28 | 57.28 |
| K2 | 25 | 29 | 47 | 4.89 | 62.17 |
| AWL | 96 | 119 | 195 | 20.27 | 82.44 |
| Other words | - | 76 | 169 | 17.57 | 100.00 |
| Words in text (tokens): 962 | | | | | |

Table 5.2 indicates the percentage of tokens (running words) in the text from each of the word lists (K1, K2, AWL) and other words (which covers technical words, numbers, proper nouns and/or low frequency words). For this text, the first thousand-word list (K1) represents 57.28 % of tokens, while the second thousand words (K2) contributes a further 4.89 %. Collectively, the first two thousand words represent 62.17 % of tokens. Beyond this use of high frequency words, the text makes use of academic words (AWL) representing 20.27 % of tokens. Remaining word use in the text categorised as *other words* is likely to include substantial use of technical words covering 17.57 % of tokens.

These data on lexical coverage (percent) of the K1, K2, AWL and *other words* in this text are reviewed in Section 5.1.5. as a summary of the four arts texts.

### 5.1.3 GenAI Jenni

The Jenni AI arts text was generated from the prompt "Bourdieu, Social Capital and Online Interaction". This text was analysed with VocabProfile with the following result output (see Table 5.3).

**Table 5.3:** VocabProfile of arts GenAI: Jenni text

| | Families | Types | Tokens | Percent (%) | Cumulative % |
|---|---|---|---|---|---|
| **K1** | 116 | 140 | 494 | 59.73 | 59.73 |
| **K2** | 16 | 18 | 27 | 3.26 | 62.99 |
| **AWL** | 72 | 93 | 165 | 19.95 | 82.94 |
| **Other words** | - | 73 | 141 | 17.05 | 100.00 |
| Words in text (tokens): 827 | | | | | |

Table 5.3 indicates the percentage of tokens (running words) in the text from each of the word lists (K1, K2, AWL) and *other words* (which covers technical words, numbers, proper nouns and/or low frequency words). For this text, the first thousand-word list (K1) represents 59.73 % of tokens, while the second thousand words (K2) contributes a further 3.26 %. Collectively, the first two thousand words represent 62.99 % of tokens. Beyond this use of high frequency words, the text makes use of academic words (AWL) representing 19.95 % of tokens. Remaining word use in the text categorised as *other words* is likely to include substantial use of technical words covering 17.05 % of tokens.

These data on lexical coverage (percent) of the K1, K2, AWL and *other words* in this text are reviewed in Section 5.1.5.

### 5.1.4 GenAI Yomu

The Yomu AI arts text was generated from the prompt "Bourdieu, Social Capital and Online Interaction". This text was analysed with VocabProfile with the following result output (see Table 5.4).

**Table 5.4:** VocabProfile of arts GenAI: Yomu text

| | Families | Types | Tokens | Percent (%) | Cumulative % |
|---|---|---|---|---|---|
| **K1** | 127 | 162 | 569 | 59.09 | 59.09 |
| **K2** | 18 | 23 | 29 | 3.01 | 62.10 |
| **AWL** | 97 | 117 | 226 | 23.47 | 85.57 |
| **Other words** | - | 75 | 139 | 14.43 | 100.00 |
| Words in text (tokens): 963 | | | | | |

Table 5.4 indicates the percentage of tokens (running words) in the text from each of the word lists (K1, K2, AWL) and *other words* (which covers technical words, numbers, proper nouns and/or low frequency words). For this text, the first thousand-word list (K1) represents 59.09 % of tokens, while the second thousand words (K2) contributes a further 3.01 %. Collectively, the first two thousand words represent 62.10 % of tokens. Beyond this use of high frequency words, the text makes use of academic words (AWL) representing 23.47 % of tokens. Remaining word use in the text categorised as *other words* is likely to include substantial use of technical words covering 14.43 % of tokens.

These data on lexical coverage (percent) of the K1, K2, AWL and *other words* in this text are reviewed in Section 5.1.5. as a summary of the four arts texts.

### 5.1.5 Comparison of Arts Texts

The lexical coverage for GSL K1, GSL K2, AWL and *other words* across the four arts texts is displayed in Table 5.5.

**Table 5.5:** VocabProfile comparison of arts texts

| Text coverage of tokens (%) | | | | |
|---|---|---|---|---|
| **(Arts)** | **Non-GenAI** | **GenAI: Scite** | **GenAI: Jenni** | **GenAI: Yomu** |
| **K1** | 71.19 | 57.28 | 59.73 | 59.09 |
| **K2** | 2.58 | 4.89 | 3.26 | 3.01 |
| **AWL** | 12.37 | 20.27 | 19.95 | 23.47 |
| **Other words** | 13.85 | 17.57 | 17.05 | 14.43 |

To summarise the data, for the three GenAI arts texts:

- The use of GSL K1 words varies between 57.28 % and 59.73 %.
- Use of GSL K2 words varies between 3.01 % and 4.89 %.
- Use of AWL words varies between 19.95 % and 23.47 %.
- Use of *other words* including many technical words varies between 14.43 % and 17.57 %.

All three GenAI arts texts make significantly less use of K1 words, and a corresponding significantly greater use of AWL words, when compared to the non-GenAI arts text.

This is visually seen in the presentation of the lexical coverage for GSL K1, GSL K2, AWL and *other words* across the four arts texts in Figure 5.1.

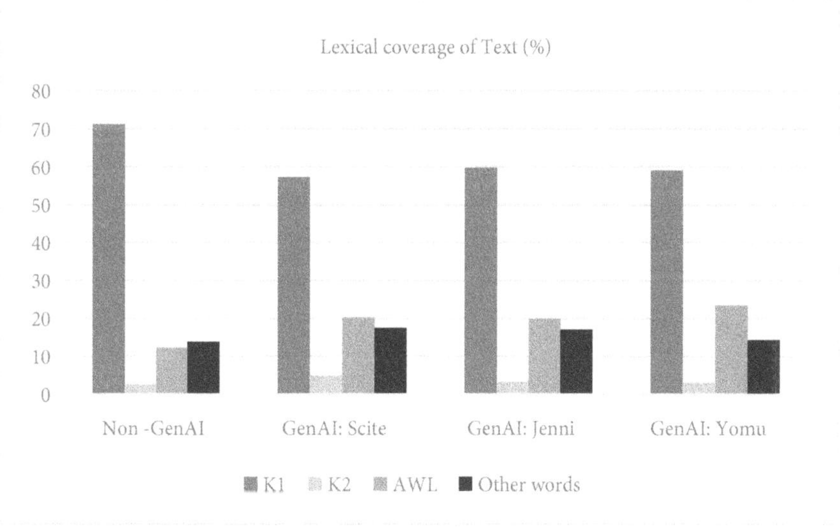


**Figure 5.1:** VocabProfile comparison of arts texts.

Let's look again at the data from the earlier study by Hirsh (2010) as a point of comparison. Hirsh (2010), in an analysis of four research articles appearing in journals covering arts, economics, law and science, found the following representation of these word lists in the texts (see Table 5.6).

**Table 5.6:** Lexical profile of four academic texts

| Text | Length (tokens) | Lexical coverage (%) | | | |
|---|---|---|---|---|---|
| | | K1 | K2 | AWL | Other words |
| Arts text | 8752 | 68.5 | 5.7 | 11.3 | 14.5 |
| Econ text | 3386 | 70.4 | 4.5 | 10.3 | 14.7 |
| Law text | 12726 | 80.8 | 4.5 | 6.4 | 8.3 |
| Sci text | 2305 | 70.0 | 5.2 | 9.7 | 15.1 |

To summarise the data, for the four academic texts:

- The use of GSL K1 words varies between 68.5 % and 80.8 %.
- Use of GSL K2 words varies between 4.5 % and 5.7 %.
- Use of AWL words varies between 6.4 % and 11.3 %.
- Use of *other words* including many technical words varies between 8.3 % and 15.1 %.

Thus, comparing the three GenAI arts texts in the current study with the four non-GenAI research papers from Hirsh (2010), the following observation can be made: that the AI-generated arts texts are making significantly greater use of academic words and correspondingly less use of the first thousand high frequency words than is the case with the four non-GenAI published research articles.

## 5.2 Commerce Texts

The following analysis is for the four commerce texts.

### 5.2.1 Non-GenAI

The non-GenAI commerce text is a research article titled *Paid Parental Leave and Children's Schooling Outcomes* published in *The Economic Journal Nature* in 2017. This text was analysed with VocabProfile with the following result output (see Table 5.7).

Table 5.7 indicates the percentage of tokens (running words) in the text from each of the word lists (K1, K2, AWL) and *other words* (which covers technical words, numbers, proper nouns and/or low frequency words). For this text, the first thousand-word list (K1) represents 74.20 % of tokens, while the second thousand words (K2) contributes a further 5.49 %. Collectively, the first two thousand words represent 79.69 % of tokens. Beyond this use of high frequency words, the text makes use of academic words (AWL) representing 10.57 % of tokens. Remaining word use in the text categorised as *other words* is likely to include substantial use of technical words covering 9.74 % of tokens.

**Table 5.7:** VocabProfile of commerce non-GenAI text

| | Families | Types | Tokens | Percent (%) | Cumulative % |
|---|---|---|---|---|---|
| K1 | 344 | 514 | 3284 | 74.20 | 74.20 |
| K2 | 65 | 87 | 243 | 5.49 | 79.69 |
| AWL | 161 | 206 | 468 | 10.57 | 90.26 |
| Other words | - | 176 | 431 | 9.74 | 100.00 |
| Words in text (tokens): 4426 | | | | | |

These data on lexical coverage (percent) of the K1, K2, AWL and *other words* in this text are reviewed in Section 5.2.5. as a summary of the four commerce texts.

### 5.2.2 GenAI Scite

The Scite AI commerce text was generated from the prompt "Paid Parental Leave and Children's Schooling Outcomes". This text was analysed with VocabProfile with the following result output (see Table 5.8).

**Table 5.8:** VocabProfile of commerce GenAI: Scite text

| | Families | Types | Tokens | Percent (%) | Cumulative % |
|---|---|---|---|---|---|
| K1 | 109 | 136 | 487 | 55.28 | 55.28 |
| K2 | 27 | 30 | 97 | 11.01 | 66.29 |
| AWL | 78 | 94 | 144 | 16.35 | 82.64 |
| Other words | - | 78 | 153 | 17.37 | 100.00 |
| Words in text (tokens): 881 | | | | | |

Table 5.8 indicates the percentage of tokens (running words) in the text from each of the word lists (K1, K2, AWL) and *other words* (which covers technical words, numbers, proper nouns and/or low frequency words). For this text, the first thousand-word list (K1) represents 55.28 % of tokens, while the second thousand words (K2) contributes a further 11.01 %. Collectively, the first two thousand words represent 66.29 % of tokens. Beyond this use of high frequency words, the text makes use of academic words (AWL) representing 16.35 % of tokens. Remaining word use in the text categorised as *other words* is likely to include substantial use of technical words covering 17.37 % of tokens.

These data on lexical coverage (percent) of the K1, K2, AWL and *other words* in this text are reviewed in Section 5.2.5. as a summary of the four commerce texts.

### 5.2.3 GenAI Jenni

The Jenni AI commerce text was generated from the prompt "Paid Parental Leave and Children's Schooling Outcomes". This text was analysed with VocabProfile with the following result output (see Table 5.9).

**Table 5.9:** VocabProfile of commerce GenAI: Jenni text

| | Families | Types | Tokens | Percent (%) | Cumulative % |
|---|---|---|---|---|---|
| K1 | 106 | 209 | 710 | 66.05 | 66.05 |
| K2 | 30 | 36 | 69 | 6.42 | 72.47 |
| AWL | 85 | 104 | 170 | 15.81 | 88.28 |
| Other words | - | 93 | 126 | 11.72 | 100.00 |
| Words in text (tokens): 1075 | | | | | |

Table 5.9 indicates the percentage of tokens (running words) in the text from each of the word lists (K1, K2, AWL) and *other words* (which covers technical words, numbers, proper nouns and/or low frequency words). For this text, the first thousand-word list (K1) represents 66.05 % of tokens, while the second thousand words (K2) contributes a further 6.42 %. Collectively, the first two thousand words represent 72.47 % of tokens. Beyond this use of high frequency words, the text makes use of academic words (AWL) representing 15.81 % of tokens. Remaining word use in the text categorised as *other words* is likely to include substantial use of technical words covering 11.72 % of tokens.

These data on lexical coverage (percent) of the K1, K2, AWL and *other words* in this text are reviewed in Section 5.2.5. as a summary of the four commerce texts.

### 5.2.4 GenAI Yomu

The Yomu AI commerce text was generated from the prompt "Paid Parental Leave and Children's Schooling Outcomes". This text was analysed with VocabProfile with the following result output (see Table 5.10).

**Table 5.10:** VocabProfile of commerce GenAI: Yomu text

| | Families | Types | Tokens | Percent (%) | Cumulative % |
|---|---|---|---|---|---|
| K1 | 170 | 208 | 616 | 61.42 | 61.42 |
| K2 | 35 | 44 | 111 | 11.07 | 72.49 |
| AWL | 106 | 128 | 210 | 20.94 | 93.43 |
| Other words | - | 54 | 66 | 6.58 | 100.00 |
| Words in text (tokens): 1003 | | | | | |

Table 5.10 indicates the percentage of tokens (running words) in the text from each of the word lists (K1, K2, AWL) and *other words* (which covers technical words, numbers, proper nouns and/or low frequency words). For this text, the first thousand-word list (K1) represents 61.42 % of tokens, while the second thousand words (K2) contributes a further 11.07 %. Collectively, the first two thousand words represent 72.49 % of tokens. Beyond this use of high frequency words, the text makes use of academic words (AWL) representing 20.94 % of tokens. Remaining word use in the text categorised as *other words* is likely to include substantial use of technical words covering 6.58 % of tokens.

These data on lexical coverage (percent) of the K1, K2, AWL and *other words* in this text are reviewed in Section 5.2.5. as a summary of the four commerce texts.

## 5.2.5 Comparison of Commerce Texts

The lexical coverage for GSL K1, GSL K2, AWL and *other words* across the four commerce texts is displayed in Table 5.11.

**Table 5.11:** VocabProfile comparison of commerce texts

| | Text coverage of tokens (%) | | | |
|---|---|---|---|---|
| | Non-GenAI | GenAI: Scite | GenAI: Jenni | GenAI: Yomu |
| K1 | 74.20 | 55.28 | 66.05 | 61.42 |
| K2 | 5.49 | 11.01 | 6.42 | 11.07 |
| AWL | 10.57 | 16.35 | 15.81 | 20.94 |
| Other words | 9.74 | 17.37 | 11.72 | 6.58 |

To summarise the data, for the three GenAI commerce texts:

- The use of GSL K1 words varies between 55.28 % and 66.05 %.
- Use of GSL K2 words varies between 6.42 % and 11.07 %.
- Use of AWL words varies between 15.81 % and 20.94 %.
- Use of *other words* including many technical words varies between 6.58 % and 17.37 %.

All three GenAI commerce texts make significantly less use of K1 words when compared to the non-GenAI commerce text, and a corresponding greater use of AWL words.

This is visually seen in the presentation of the lexical coverage for GSL K1, GSL K2, AWL and *other words* across the four commerce texts in Figure 5.2.

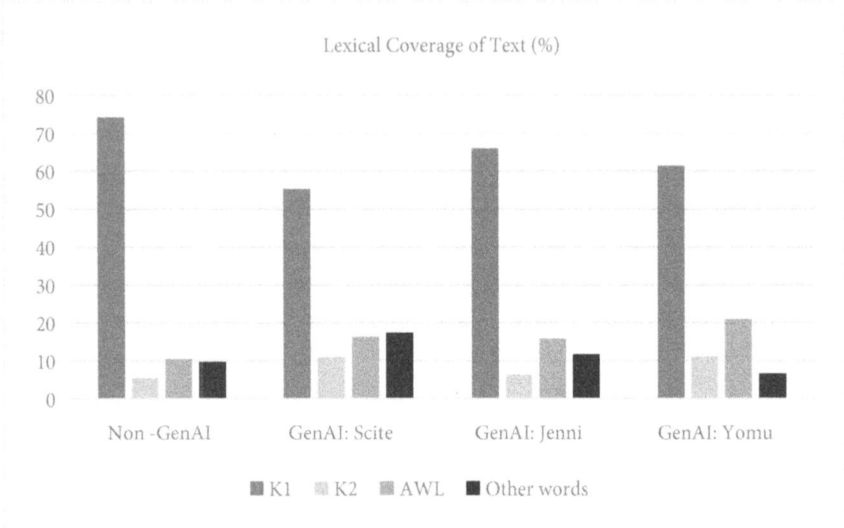


**Figure 5.2:** VocabProfile comparison of commerce texts.

Let's look again at the data from the earlier study by Hirsh (2010) as a point of comparison. Hirsh (2010), in an analysis of four research articles appearing in journals covering arts, economics, law and science, found the following representation of these word lists in the texts (see Table 5.12).

**Table 5.12:** Lexical profile of four academic texts

| Text | Length (tokens) | Lexical coverage (%) | | | |
|---|---|---|---|---|---|
| | | K1 | K2 | AWL | Other words |
| Arts text | 8752 | 68.5 | 5.7 | 11.3 | 14.5 |
| Econ text | 3386 | 70.4 | 4.5 | 10.3 | 14.7 |
| Law text | 12726 | 80.8 | 4.5 | 6.4 | 8.3 |
| Sci text | 2305 | 70.0 | 5.2 | 9.7 | 15.1 |

To summarise the data, for the four academic texts:

- The use of GSL K1 words varies between 68.5 % and 80.8 %.
- Use of GSL K2 words varies between 4.5 % and 5.7 %.
- Use of AWL words varies between 6.4 % and 11.3 %.
- Use of *other words* including many technical words varies between 8.3 % and 15.1 %.

Thus, comparing the three GenAI commerce texts in the current study with the four non-GenAI research papers from Hirsh (2010), the following observation can be made: that the three AI-generated commerce texts are making significantly greater use of academic words and an overall trend across the three texts of less use of the first thousand high frequency words than is the case with the four non-GenAI published research articles.

## 5.3 Law Texts

The following analysis is for the four law texts.

### 5.3.1 Non-GenAI

The non-GenAI law text is a research article titled *Anti-Social Behaviour, Behavioural Expectations and an Urban Aesthetic* published in *The British Journal of Criminology* in 2008. This text was analysed with VocabProfile with the following result output (see Table 5.13).

**Table 5.13:** VocabProfile of law non-GenAI text

| | Families | Types | Tokens | Percent (%) | Cumulative % |
|---|---|---|---|---|---|
| K1 | 469 | 717 | 4186 | 72.40 | 72.40 |
| K2 | 118 | 152 | 321 | 5.55 | 77.95 |
| AWL | 175 | 258 | 432 | 7.47 | 85.42 |
| Other words | - | 389 | 843 | 14.58 | 100.00 |
| Words in text (tokens): 5782 | | | | | |

Table 5.13 indicates the percentage of tokens (running words) in the text from each of the word lists (K1, K2, AWL) and *other words* (which covers technical words, numbers, proper nouns and/or low frequency words). For this text, the first thousand-word list (K1) represents 72.40 % of tokens, while the second thousand words (K2) contributes a further 5.55 %. Collectively, the first two thousand words represent 77.95 % of tokens. Beyond this use of high frequency words, the text makes use of academic words (AWL) representing 7.47 % of tokens. Remaining word use in the text categorised as *other words* is likely to include substantial use of technical words covering 14.58 % of tokens.

These data on lexical coverage (percent) of the K1, K2, AWL and *other words* in this text are reviewed in Section 5.3.5. as a summary of the four law texts.

## 5.3.2 GenAI Scite

The Scite AI law text was generated from the prompt "Anti-Social Behaviour, Behavioural Expectations and an Urban Aesthetic". This text was analysed with VocabProfile with the following result output (see Table 5.14).

**Table 5.14:** VocabProfile of law GenAI: Scite text

| | Families | Types | Tokens | Percent (%) | Cumulative % |
|---|---|---|---|---|---|
| K1 | 131 | 157 | 551 | 57.28 | 57.28 |
| K2 | 25 | 29 | 47 | 4.89 | 62.17 |
| AWL | 96 | 119 | 195 | 20.27 | 82.44 |
| Other words | - | 76 | 169 | 17.57 | 100.00 |
| Words in text (tokens): 962 | | | | | |

Table 5.14 indicates the percentage of tokens (running words) in the text from each of the word lists (K1, K2, AWL) and *other words* (which covers technical words, numbers, proper nouns and/or low frequency words). For this text, the first thousand-word list (K1) represents 57.28 % of tokens, while the second thousand words (K2) contributes a further 4.89 %. Collectively, the first two thousand words represent 62.17 % of tokens. Beyond this use of high frequency words, the text makes use of academic words (AWL) representing 20.27 % of tokens. Remaining word use in the text categorised as *other words* is likely to include substantial use of technical words covering 17.57 % of tokens.

These data on lexical coverage (percent) of the K1, K2, AWL and *other words* in this text are reviewed in Section 5.3.5. as a summary of the four law texts.

## 5.3.3 GenAI Jenni

The Jenni AI law text was generated from the prompt "Anti-Social Behaviour, Behavioural Expectations and an Urban Aesthetic". This text was analysed with VocabProfile with the following result output (see Table 5.15).

**Table 5.15:** VocabProfile of law GenAI: Jenni text

| | Families | Types | Tokens | Percent (%) | Cumulative % |
|---|---|---|---|---|---|
| K1 | 150 | 193 | 683 | 57.64 | 57.64 |
| K2 | 28 | 34 | 45 | 3.80 | 61.44 |
| AWL | 104 | 136 | 233 | 19.66 | 81.10 |
| Other words | - | 132 | 224 | 18.90 | 100.00 |
| Words in text (tokens): 1185 | | | | | |

Table 5.15 indicates the percentage of tokens (running words) in the text from each of the word lists (K1, K2, AWL) and *other words* (which covers technical words, numbers, proper nouns and/or low frequency words). For this text, the first thousand-word list (K1) represents 57.64 % of tokens, while the second thousand words (K2) contributes a further 3.80 %. Collectively, the first two thousand words represent 61.44 % of tokens. Beyond this use of high frequency words, the text makes use of academic words (AWL) representing 19.66 % of tokens. Remaining word use in the text categorised as *other words* is likely to include substantial use of technical words covering 18.90 % of tokens.

These data on lexical coverage (percent) of the K1, K2, AWL and *other words* in this text are reviewed in Section 5.3.5. as a summary of the four law texts.

### 5.3.4 GenAI Yomu

The Yomu AI law text was generated from the prompt "Anti-Social Behaviour, Behavioural Expectations and an Urban Aesthetic". This text was analysed with VocabProfile with the following result output (see Table 5.16).

**Table 5.16:** VocabProfile of law GenAI: Yomu text

| | Families | Types | Tokens | Percent (%) | Cumulative % |
|---|---|---|---|---|---|
| K1 | 125 | 143 | 481 | 55.29 | 55.29 |
| K2 | 25 | 30 | 76 | 8.74 | 64.03 |
| AWL | 74 | 91 | 157 | 18.05 | 82.08 |
| Other words | - | 66 | 156 | 17.93 | 100.00 |
| Words in text (tokens): 870 | | | | | |

Table 5.16 indicates the percentage of tokens (running words) in the text from each of the word lists (K1, K2, AWL) and *other words* (which covers technical words, numbers, proper nouns and/or low frequency words). For this text, the first thousand-word list (K1) represents 55.29 % of tokens, while the second thousand words (K2) contributes a further 8.74 %. Collectively, the first two thousand words represent 64.03 % of tokens. Beyond this use of high frequency words, the text makes use of academic words (AWL) representing 18.05 % of tokens. Remaining word use in the text categorised as *other words* is likely to include substantial use of technical words covering 17.93 % of tokens.

These data on lexical coverage (percent) of the K1, K2, AWL and *other words* in this text are reviewed in Section 5.3.5. as a summary of the four law texts.

### 5.3.5 Comparison of Law Texts

The lexical coverage for GSL K1, GSL K2, AWL and *other words* across the four law texts is displayed in Table 5.17.

**Table 5.17:** VocabProfile comparison of law texts

| | Text coverage of tokens (%) | | | |
|---|---|---|---|---|
| | Non-GenAI | GenAI: Scite | GenAI: Jenni | GenAI: Yomu |
| K1 | 72.40 | 57.28 | 57.64 | 55.29 |
| K2 | 5.55 | 4.89 | 3.80 | 8.74 |
| AWL | 7.47 | 20.27 | 19.66 | 18.05 |
| Other words | 14.58 | 17.57 | 18.90 | 17.93 |

To summarise the data, for the three GenAI law texts:

- The use of GSL K1 words varies between 55.29 % and 57.64 %.
- Use of GSL K2 words varies between 3.80 % and 8.74 %.
- Use of AWL words varies between 18.05 % and 20.27 %.
- Use of *other words* including many technical words varies between 17.57 % and 18.90 %.

All three GenAI law texts make significantly less use of K1 words, and a corresponding significantly greater use of AWL words, when compared to the non-GenAI law text.

This is visually seen in the presentation of the lexical coverage for GSL K1, GSL K2, AWL and *other words* across the four law texts in Figure 5.3.

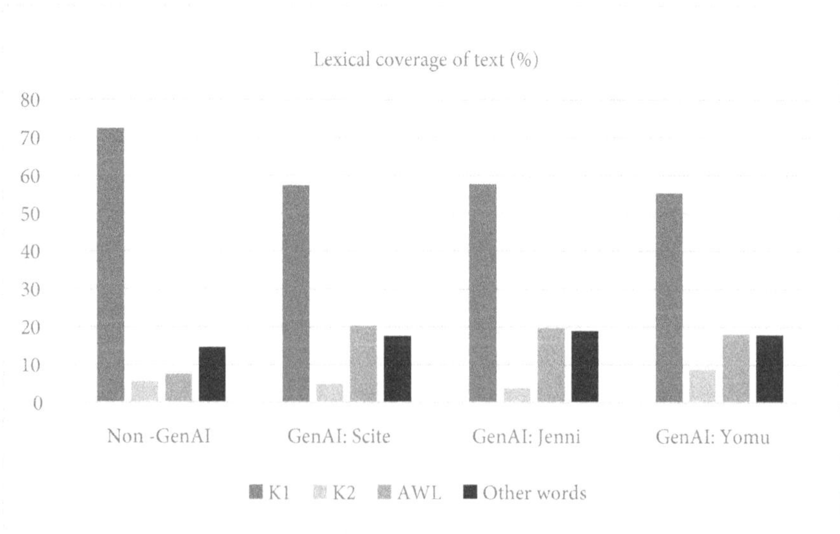


**Figure 5.3:** VocabProfile comparison of law texts.

Looking again at the data from the earlier study by Hirsh (2010) as a point of comparison, Hirsh (2010), in an analysis of four research articles appearing in journals covering arts, economics law and science, found the following representation of these word lists in the texts (see Table 5.18).

**Table 5.18:** Lexical profile of four academic texts

| Text | Length (tokens) | Lexical coverage (%) | | | |
|---|---|---|---|---|---|
| | | K1 | K2 | AWL | Other words |
| Arts text | 8752 | 68.5 | 5.7 | 11.3 | 14.5 |
| Econ text | 3386 | 70.4 | 4.5 | 10.3 | 14.7 |
| Law text | 12726 | 80.8 | 4.5 | 6.4 | 8.3 |
| Sci text | 2305 | 70.0 | 5.2 | 9.7 | 15.1 |

To summarise the data, for the four academic texts:

- The use of GSL K1 words varies between 68.5 % and 80.8 %.
- Use of GSL K2 words varies between 4.5 % and 5.7 %.
- Use of AWL words varies between 6.4 % and 11.3 %.
- Use of *other words* including many technical words varies between 8.3 % and 15.1 %.

Thus, comparing the three GenAI law texts in the current study with the four non-GenAI research papers from Hirsh (2010), the following observation can be made: that the AI-generated law texts are making significantly greater use of academic words and correspondingly less use of the first thousand high frequency words than is the case with the four non-GenAI published research articles.

## 5.4 Science Texts

The following analysis is for the four science texts.

### 5.4.1 Non-GenAI

The non-GenAI science text is a research article titled *Risk of Yellow Fever Virus Transmission in the Asia-Pacific Region* published in *Nature Communications* in 2020. This text was analysed with VocabProfile with the following result output (see Table 5.19).

**Table 5.19:** VocabProfile of science non-GenAI text

| | Families | Types | Tokens | Percent (%) | Cumulative % |
|---|---|---|---|---|---|
| K1 | 261 | 339 | 1958 | 57.50 | 57.50 |
| K2 | 55 | 70 | 150 | 4.41 | 61.91 |
| AWL | 100 | 137 | 277 | 8.14 | 70.05 |
| Other words | - | 265 | 1020 | 29.96 | 100.00 |
| Words in text (tokens): 3405 | | | | | |

Table 5.19 indicates the percentage of tokens (running words) in the text from each of the word lists (K1, K2, AWL) and *other words* (which covers technical words, numbers, proper nouns and/or low frequency words). For this text, the first thousand-word list (K1) represents 57.50 % of tokens, while the second thousand words (K2) contributes a further 4.41 %. Collectively, the first two thousand words represent 61.91 % of tokens. Beyond this use of high frequency words, the text makes use of academic words (AWL) representing 8.14 % of tokens. Remaining word use in the text categorised as *other words* is likely to include substantial use of technical words covering 29.96 % of tokens.

These data on lexical coverage (percent) of the K1, K2, AWL and *other words* in this text are reviewed in Section 5.4.5. as a summary of the four science texts.

### 5.4.2 GenAI Scite

The Scite AI science text was generated from the prompt "Risk of Yellow Fever Virus Transmission in the Asia-Pacific Region". This text was analysed with VocabProfile with the following result output (see Table 5.20).

**Table 5.20:** VocabProfile of science GenAI: Scite text

| | Families | Types | Tokens | Percent (%) | Cumulative % |
|---|---|---|---|---|---|
| K1 | 110 | 132 | 358 | 48.64 | 48.64 |
| K2 | 18 | 20 | 62 | 8.42 | 57.06 |
| AWL | 54 | 65 | 101 | 13.72 | 70.78 |
| Other words | - | 105 | 215 | 29.21 | 100.00 |
| Words in text (tokens): 736 | | | | | |

Table 5.20 indicates the percentage of tokens (running words) in the text from each of the word lists (K1, K2, AWL) and *other words* (which covers technical words, numbers, proper nouns and/or low frequency words). For this text, the first thousand-word list (K1) represents 48.64 % of tokens, while the second thousand words (K2) contributes a further 8.42 %. Collectively, the first two thousand words

represent 57.06 % of tokens. Beyond this use of high frequency words, the text makes use of academic words (AWL) representing 13.72 % of tokens. Remaining word use in the text categorised as *other words* is likely to include substantial use of technical words covering 29.21 % of tokens.

These data on lexical coverage (percent) of the K1, K2, AWL and *other words* in this text are reviewed in Section 5.4.5. as a summary of the four science texts.

### 5.4.3 GenAI Jenni

The Jenni AI science text was generated from the prompt "Risk of Yellow Fever Virus Transmission in the Asia-Pacific Region". This text was analysed with VocabProfile with the following result output (see Table 5.21).

**Table 5.21:** VocabProfile of science GenAI: Jenni text

| | Families | Types | Tokens | Percent (%) | Cumulative % |
|---|---|---|---|---|---|
| K1 | 114 | 143 | 429 | 53.76 | 53.76 |
| K2 | 26 | 27 | 67 | 8.40 | 62.16 |
| AWL | 63 | 68 | 129 | 16.17 | 78.33 |
| Other words | - | 89 | 173 | 21.68 | 100.00 |
| Words in text (tokens): 798 | | | | | |

Table 5.21 indicates the percentage of tokens (running words) in the text from each of the word lists (K1, K2, AWL) and *other words* (which covers technical words, numbers, proper nouns and/or low frequency words). For this text, the first thousand-word list (K1) represents 53.76 % of tokens, while the second thousand words (K2) contributes a further 8.40 %. Collectively, the first two thousand words represent 62.16 % of tokens. Beyond this use of high frequency words, the text makes use of academic words (AWL) representing 16.17 % of tokens. Remaining word use in the text categorised as *other words* is likely to include substantial use of technical words covering 21.68 % of tokens.

These data on lexical coverage (percent) of the K1, K2, AWL and *other words* in this text are reviewed in Section 5.4.5. as a summary of the four science texts.

### 5.4.4 GenAI Yomu

The Yomu AI science text was generated from the prompt "Risk of Yellow Fever Virus Transmission in the Asia-Pacific Region". This text was analysed with VocabProfile with the following result output (see Table 5.22).

**Table 5.22:** VocabProfile of science GenAI: Yomu text

| | Families | Types | Tokens | Percent (%) | Cumulative % |
|---|---|---|---|---|---|
| K1 | 133 | 163 | 467 | 52.41 | 52.41 |
| K2 | 31 | 36 | 91 | 10.21 | 62.62 |
| AWL | 66 | 79 | 143 | 16.05 | 78.67 |
| Other words | - | 105 | 190 | 21.32 | 100.00 |
| Words in text (tokens): 891 | | | | | |

Table 5.22 indicates the percentage of tokens (running words) in the text from each of the word lists (K1, K2, AWL) and *other words* (which covers technical words, numbers, proper nouns and/or low frequency words). For this text, the first thousand-word list (K1) represents 52.41 % of tokens, while the second thousand words (K2) contributes a further 10.21 %. Collectively, the first two thousand words represent 62.62 % of tokens. Beyond this use of high frequency words, the text makes use of academic words (AWL) representing 16.05 % of tokens. Remaining word use in the text categorised as *other words* is likely to include substantial use of technical words covering 21.32 % of tokens.

These data on lexical coverage (percent) of the K1, K2, AWL and *other words* in this text are reviewed in Section 5.4.5. as a summary of the four science texts.

### 5.4.5 Comparison of Science Texts

The lexical coverage for GSL K1, GSL K2, AWL and *other words* across the four science texts is displayed in Table 5.23.

**Table 5.23:** VocabProfile comparison of science texts

| | Text coverage of tokens (%) | | | |
|---|---|---|---|---|
| | Non-GenAI | GenAI: Scite | GenAI: Jenni | GenAI: Yomu |
| K1 | 57.50 | 48.64 | 53.76 | 52.41 |
| K2 | 4.41 | 8.42 | 8.40 | 10.21 |
| AWL | 8.14 | 13.72 | 16.17 | 16.05 |
| Other words | 29.96 | 29.21 | 21.68 | 21.32 |

To summarise the data, for the three GenAI science texts:

- The use of GSL K1 words varies between 48.64 % and 53.76 %.
- Use of GSL K2 words varies between 8.40 % and 10.21 %.
- Use of AWL words varies between 13.72 % and 16.17 %.
- Use of *other words* including many technical words varies between 21.32 % and 29.21 %.

The lexical profile of the three GenAI science texts displays some greater use of K2 words and also AWL words when compared to the non-GenAI science text.

This is visually seen in the presentation of the lexical coverage for GSL K1, GSL K2, AWL and *other words* across the four science texts in Figure 5.4.

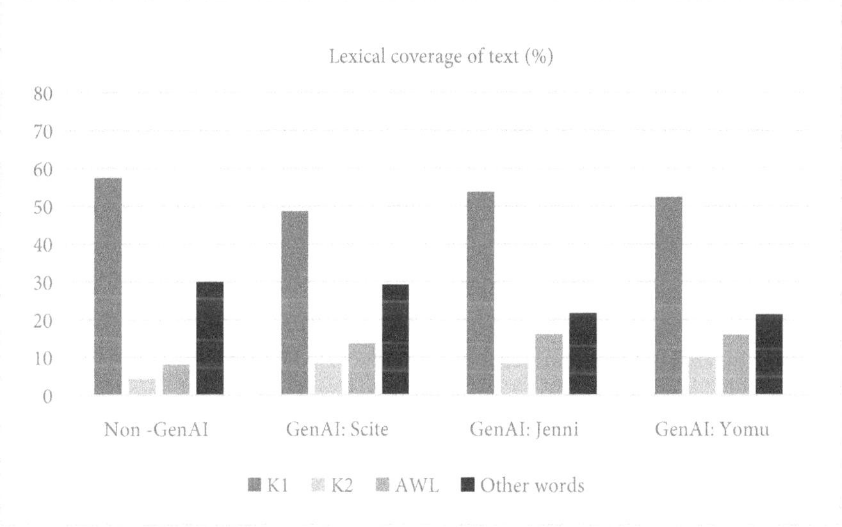


**Figure 5.4:** VocabProfile comparison of science texts.

Let's look again at the data from the earlier study by Hirsh (2010) as a point of comparison. Hirsh (2010), in an analysis of four research articles appearing in journals covering arts, economics, law and science, found the following representation of these word lists in the texts (see Table 5.24).

**Table 5.24:** Lexical profile of four academic texts

| Text | Length (tokens) | Lexical coverage (%) | | | |
|---|---|---|---|---|---|
| | | K1 | K2 | AWL | Other words |
| Arts text | 8752 | 68.5 | 5.7 | 11.3 | 14.5 |
| Econ text | 3386 | 70.4 | 4.5 | 10.3 | 14.7 |
| Law text | 12726 | 80.8 | 4.5 | 6.4 | 8.3 |
| Sci text | 2305 | 70.0 | 5.2 | 9.7 | 15.1 |

To summarise the data, for the four academic texts:

- The use of GSL K1 words varies between 68.5 % and 80.8 %.
- Use of GSL K2 words varies between 4.5 % and 5.7 %.
- Use of AWL words varies between 6.4 % and 11.3 %.
- Use of *other words* including many technical words varies between 8.3 % and 15.1 %.

Thus, comparing the three GenAI science texts in the current study with the four non-GenAI research papers from Hirsh (2010), the following observation can be made: that the AI-generated science texts are making significantly greater use of K2 words and academic words and correspondingly less use of the first thousand high frequency words than is the case with the four non-GenAI published research articles.

# 6. Analysis 2: K1 to K10 Words

This chapter presents a lexical analysis of the non-GenAI text and the three GenAI texts, with separate reporting for arts, commerce, law and science. The analysis displays the lexical coverage as percentage (%) for the following groups of words:

- BNC-COCA: K1 to K10

The words in these word lists are grouped as word families.

## 6.1 Arts Texts

The analysis displayed in Table 6.1 is for the four arts texts.

**Table 6.1:** K1-K10 words in arts texts

| | non-GenAI | GenAI Scite | GenAI Jenni | GenAI Yomu |
|---|---|---|---|---|
| K1 | 69.48 | 54.25 | 54.65 | 51.07 |
| K2 | 13.88 | 22.12 | 20.85 | 23.75 |
| K3 | 10.77 | 16.22 | 16.02 | 18.86 |
| K4 | 1.83 | 3.40 | 3.89 | 2.75 |
| K5 | 0.48 | 1.20 | 1.53 | 1.53 |
| K6 | 0.24 | 0.50 | 0.12 | 1.22 |
| K7 | 0.37 | 0.30 | 0.35 | 0.31 |
| K8 | 0.25 | 0.60 | 0.47 | 0.10 |
| K9 | 0.14 | 0.10 | 0.24 | 0 |
| K10 | 0.13 | 0 | 0 | 0.10 |

Table 6.1 indicates that the non-GenAI arts text use of the first thousand words of the BNC-COCA corpus (K1) is 69.48 % of tokens (running words), significantly higher than K1 use in GenAI Scite (54.25 %), GenAI Jenni (54.65 %) and GenAI Yomu (51.07 %). The non-GenAI text use of the second thousand words of the BNC-COCA corpus (K2) is 13.88 % of tokens (running words), significantly lower than K2 use in GenAI Scite (22.12 %), GenAI Jenni (20.85 %) and GenAI Yomu (23.75 %). This pattern is also evident for the third thousand words of the BNC-COCA corpus (K3), with less use of K3 words in the non-GenAI text (10.77 %) when compared with GenAI Scite (16.22 %), GenAI Jenni (16.02 %) and GenAI Yomu (18.86 %). Beyond K3, word use of K4 to K10 words becomes noticeably reduced for all four texts with minimal significant differences across the four texts.

Thus, from the raw data, it is evident that the three GenAI arts texts make less use of K1 words than the non-GenAI arts text and, correspondingly, make greater use of K2 and K3 words than is the case with the non-GenAI text. This pattern is visually evident in Figure 6.1.

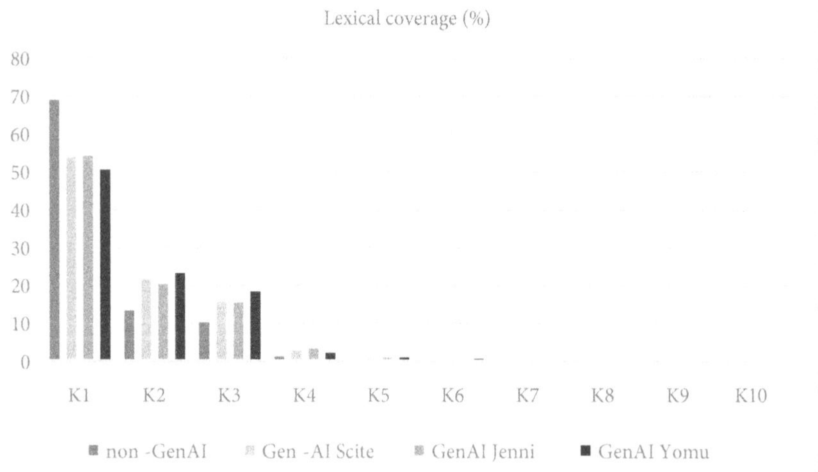


**Figure 6.1:** K1-K10 words in arts texts.

The suggestion from the data is that the three GenAI arts texts are quite similar in lexical profile, and also noticeably different from the non-GenAI arts text.

## 6.2 Commerce Texts

The analysis displayed in Table 6.2 is for the four commerce texts.

**Table 6.2:** K1-K10 words in commerce texts

| | non-GenAI | Gen-AI Scite | GenAI Jenni | GenAI Yomu |
|---|---|---|---|---|
| K1 | 72.24 | 61.81 | 67.37 | 62.74 |
| K2 | 11.03 | 15.03 | 16.27 | 17.78 |
| K3 | 9.40 | 12.43 | 9.93 | 14.89 |
| K4 | 2.57 | 4.41 | 2.76 | 1.90 |
| K5 | 1.54 | 15.8 | 0.64 | 0.80 |
| K6 | 0.21 | 0.57 | 0.55 | 0.80 |
| K7 | 0.16 | 0.90 | 0.37 | 0.30 |
| K8 | 0.05 | 0.23 | 0 | 0.10 |
| K9 | 0.07 | 0.11 | 0.09 | 0 |
| K10 | 0.07 | 0 | 0.09 | 0 |

Table 6.2 indicates that the non-GenAI commerce text use of the first thousand words of the BNC-COCA corpus (K1) is 72.24 % of tokens (running words), marginally higher overall than K1 use in GenAI Scite (61.81 %), GenAI Jenni (67.37 %) and GenAI Yomu (62.74 %). The non-GenAI text use of the second thousand words of the BNC-COCA corpus (K2) is 11.03 % of tokens (running words), marginally lower than K2 use in GenAI Scite (15.03 %), GenAI Jenni (16.27 %) and GenAI Yomu (17.78 %). For the third thousand words of the BNC-COCA corpus (K3), word use is comparable across the four texts, seen in non-GenAI text (9.40 %) when compared with GenAI Scite (12.43 %), GenAI Jenni (9.93 %) and GenAI Yomu (14.89 %). Beyond K3, word use of K4 to K10 words becomes noticeably reduced for all four texts with minimal significant differences across the four texts.

Thus, from the raw data, it is evident that the three GenAI commerce texts make slightly less use of K1 words than the non-GenAI commerce text and, correspondingly, make slightly greater use of K2 words than is the case with the non-GenAI text.

The suggestion from the data in Figure 6.2 is that the three GenAI commerce texts display generally similar profiles to the non-GenAI commerce text with slight differences noted between the three GenAI texts and the non-GenAI text in use of K1 and K2 words.

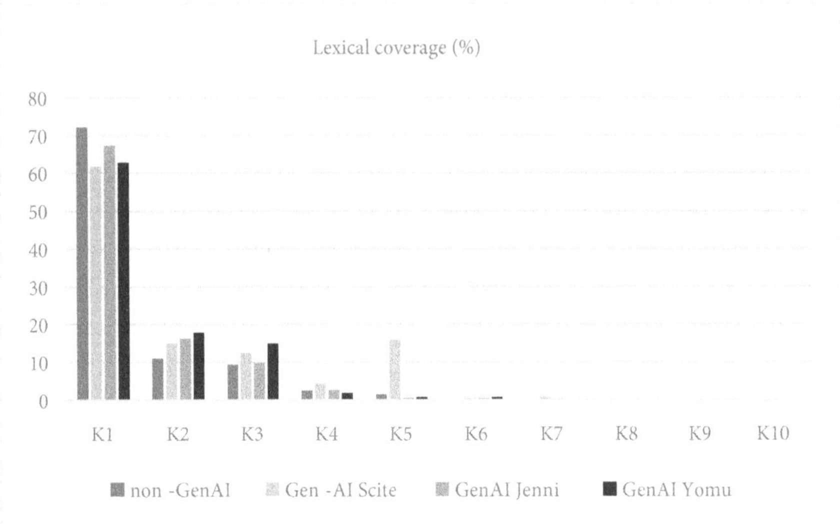


**Figure 6.2:** K1-K10 words in commerce texts.

## 6.3 Law Texts

The analysis displayed in Table 6.3 is for the four law texts.

**Table 6.3:** K1-K10 words in law texts

| | non-GenAI | Gen-AI Scite | GenAI Jenni | GenAI Yomu |
|---|---|---|---|---|
| K1 | 73.61 | 47.14 | 57.41 | 50.40 |
| K2 | 9.77 | 21.24 | 15.57 | 16.53 |
| K3 | 8.80 | 19.05 | 16.75 | 20.55 |
| K4 | 3.17 | 5.81 | 5.39 | 6.43 |
| K5 | 0.74 | 1.52 | 1.35 | 1.03 |
| K6 | 0.62 | 0.76 | 0.67 | 1.49 |
| K7 | 0.93 | 1.05 | 0.17 | 0.57 |
| K8 | 0.29 | 0.57 | 0.67 | 0.46 |
| K9 | 0.19 | 0.19 | 0.08 | 0 |
| K10 | 0.10 | 0.10 | 0 | 0 |

Table 6.3 indicates that the non-GenAI law text use of the first thousand words of the BNC-COCA corpus (K1) is 73.61 % of tokens (running words), significantly higher than K1 use in GenAI Scite (47.14 %), GenAI Jenni (57.41 %) and GenAI Yomu (50.40 %). The non-GenAI text use of the second thousand words of the BNC-COCA corpus (K2) is 9.77 % of tokens (running words), significantly lower than K2 use in GenAI Scite (21.24 %), GenAI Jenni (15.57 %) and GenAI Yomu (16.53 %). This pattern is evident for the third thousand words of the BNC-COCA corpus (K3), where there is significantly less use of K3 words in the non-GenAI text (8.80 %) when compared with GenAI Scite (19.05 %), GenAI Jenni (16.75 %) and GenAI Yomu (20.55 %). Beyond K3, word use of K4 to K10 words becomes greatly reduced for all four texts with minimal significant differences across the four texts.

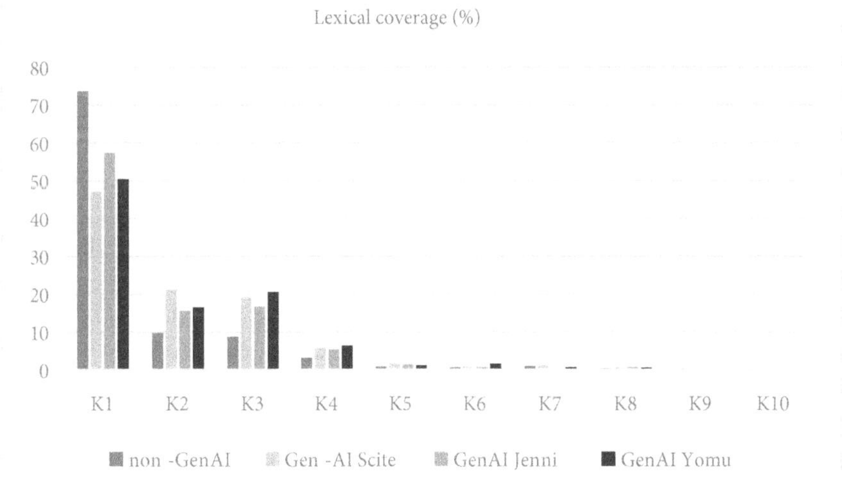


**Figure 6.3:** K1-K10 words in law texts.

Thus, from the raw data, it is evident that the three GenAI law texts make considerably less use of K1 words than the non-GenAI law text and, correspondingly, make considerably greater use of both K2 words and K3 words than is the case with the non-GenAI text. This pattern is visually evident in Figure 6.3.

The suggestion from the data is that the three GenAI law texts are quite similar in lexical profile, and also noticeably different from the non-GenAI law text.

## 6.4 Science Texts

The analysis displayed in Table 6.4 is for the four science texts.

**Table 6.4:** K1-K10 words in science texts

| | non-GenAI | Gen-AI Scite | GenAI Jenni | GenAI Yomu |
|---|---|---|---|---|
| K1 | 67.43 | 53.67 | 54.67 | 54.73 |
| K2 | 9.14 | 12.36 | 16.07 | 17.13 |
| K3 | 9.97 | 14.81 | 15.44 | 15.91 |
| K4 | 2.42 | 6.25 | 3.86 | 3.45 |
| K5 | 2.93 | 3.26 | 2.86 | 3.45 |
| K6 | 1.91 | 3.53 | 2.74 | 2.34 |
| K7 | 1.70 | 0.68 | 0.25 | 0.33 |
| K8 | 0.65 | 1.09 | 0.75 | 1.22 |
| K9 | 0.11 | 0.14 | 0.25 | 0.11 |
| K10 | 0.07 | 0 | 0.13 | 0.11 |

Table 6.4 indicates that the non-GenAI science text use of the first thousand words of the BNC-COCA corpus (K1) is 67.43 % of tokens (running words), noticeably higher than K1 use in GenAI Scite (53.67 %), GenAI Jenni (54.67 %) and GenAI Yomu (54.73 %). The non-GenAI text use of the second thousand words of the BNC-COCA corpus (K2) is 9.14 % of tokens (running words), slightly lower overall than K2 use in GenAI Scite (12.36 %), GenAI Jenni (16.07 %) and GenAI Yomu (17.13 %). This pattern is also evident for the third thousand words of the BNC-COCA corpus (K3), with less use of K3 words in the non-GenAI text (9.97 %) when compared with GenAI Scite (14.81 %), GenAI Jenni (15.44 %) and GenAI Yomu (15.91 %). Beyond K3, word use of K4 to K10 words becomes noticeably reduced for all four texts with minimal significant differences across the four texts.

Thus, from the raw data, it is evident that the three GenAI science texts make less use of K1 words than the non-GenAI science text and, correspondingly, make slightly greater use of K2 and K3 words than is the case with the non-GenAI text. This pattern is visually evident in Figure 6.4.

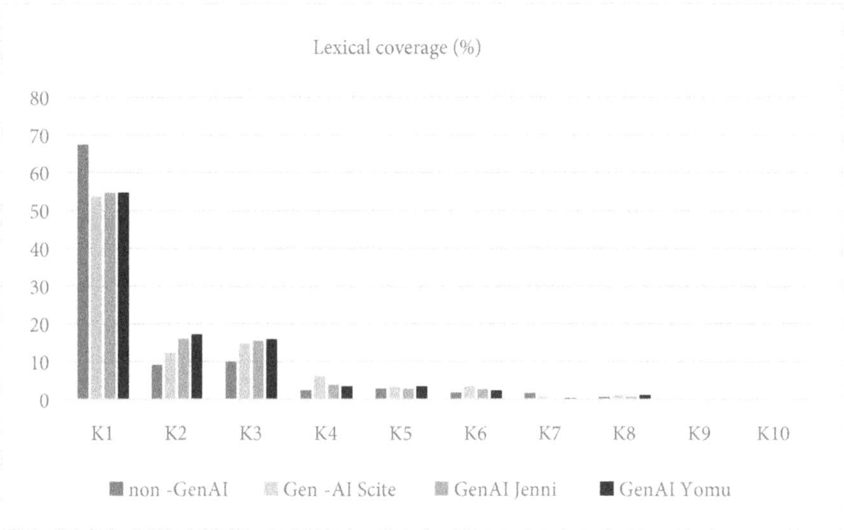


**Figure 6.4:** K1-K10 words in science texts.

The suggestion from the data is that the three GenAI science texts are quite similar in lexical profile, and also slightly different from the non-GenAI science text.

# 7. Analysis 3: 20 Most Frequently Occurring Content Words

This chapter presents the most frequently occurring content words in the non-GenAI text and the three GenAI texts, with separate reporting for arts, commerce, law and science. The words in these lists are grouped as word families, and reported in decreasing frequency of occurrence, with the most frequently occurring content word listed first. Function words (e.g., *the, of, at, in, and, but*) are excluded. As numerical data appearing in the texts (in the form of numbers, statistics and citation dates) are reported as 'number', this item is removed from the reporting. The resulting lists capture the key subject-specific vocabulary of each text.

## 7.1 Arts Texts

The following analysis is for the four arts texts. The 20 most frequently occurring word families (excluding function words) are reported in Table 7.1 in descending order of frequency of occurrence.

**Table 7.1:** Top 20 content words in arts texts

| ARTS | | | |
|---|---|---|---|
| **Non-GenAI** | **GenAI Scite** | **GenAI Jenni** | **GenAI Yomu** |
| social | social | social | social |
| capital | capital | capital | capital |
| Bourdieu | online | online | online |
| online | interactions | digital | Bourdieu |
| digital | individuals | individuals | cultural |
| interactions | connections | field | networks |
| internet | digital | Bourdieu | digital |
| individuals | Bourdieu | cultural | interactions |
| memes | networks | interactions | individuals |
| habitus | relationships | networks | platforms |
| American | platforms | resources | access |
| field | bridging | understanding | media |
| meme | communication | access | traditional |
| knowledge | ties | concepts | challenges |
| distinction | bonding | connections | network |
| good | communities | dynamics | relationships |
| group | Lee | economic | concept |
| information | offline | habitus | implications |
| inhabitants | resources | outcomes | interaction |
| new | studies | platforms | leverage |

It is evident in the data that all four texts share a degree of similarity in the use of content words, with the following five words appearing high on the lists for all four arts texts: *social, capital, online, digital, Bourdieu.* There are also some differences evident across the four arts texts in content word use which appears to reflect the social construction of language, giving the writing human-like qualities in terms of construction of ideas.

## 7.2 Commerce Texts

The following analysis is for the four commerce texts. The 20 most frequently occurring word families (excluding function words) are reported in Table 7.2 in descending order of frequency of occurrence.

**Table 7.2:** Top 20 content words in commerce texts

| COM | | | |
|---|---|---|---|
| **Non-GenAI** | **GenAI Scite** | **GenAI Jenni** | **GenAI Yomu** |
| leave | leave | leave | parental |
| child | child | paid | leave |
| effect | parental | family | child |
| mother | educational | child | educational |
| parental | paid | policy | paid |
| maternal | health | parental | early |
| reform | outcome | outcome | policy |
| time | academic | schooling | outcome |
| care | policy | parent | development |
| outcome | better | development | family |
| month | family | support | benefit |
| employment | improve | effect | parent |
| work | availability | employment | impact |
| development | development | impact | attainment |
| extension | maternal | early | support |
| income | often | improve | challenge |
| labour | readiness | maternal | crucial |
| birth | social | potentially | diverse |
| cognitive | broader | work | effect |
| study | consider | attainment | factor |

It is evident in the data that all four texts share a degree of similarity in the use of content words, with the following four words appearing high on the lists: *leave, child, parental, outcome.* These words convey some of the core subject matter suggested in the paper title and GenAI prompt. There are also some differences evident across the four commerce texts in content word use which appears to reflect the social construction of language, giving the writing human-like qualities in terms of construction of ideas.

## 7.3 Law Texts

The following analysis is for the four law texts. The 20 most frequently occurring word families (excluding function words) are reported in Table 7.3 in descending order of frequency of occurrence.

**Table 7.3:** Top 20 content words in law texts

| LAW | | | |
|---|---|---|---|
| **Non-GenAI** | **GenAI Scite** | **GenAI Jenni** | **GenAI Yomu** |
| behaviour | social | urban | urban |
| social | behaviour | environment | social |
| asb | urban | aesthetic | behavior |
| graffiti | aesthetic | design | aesthetic |
| people | community | space | norm |
| urban | expectation | social | space |
| aesthetic | environment | nature | community |
| criminal | space | landscape | public |
| group | positive | building | cultural |
| young | public | cultural | environment |
| city | creating | experience | area |
| expectation | foster | physical | community |
| activity | interaction | planning | expectation |
| context | resident | ecological | inclusivity |
| different | design | green | local |
| order | engagement | human | value |
| see | norms | architecture | visual |
| according | conduct | art | activity |
| instance | often | behavior | balance |
| public | participation | city | city |

It is evident in the data that all four texts share a degree of similarity in the use of content words, with the following four words appearing high on the lists: *social, behaviour, aesthetic, urban.* Other content words occur in three texts, including: *city, public.* Collectively, these words convey the core subject matter suggested in the paper title and GenAI prompt. There are also some differences evident across the four law texts in content word use which appears to reflect the social construction of language, giving the writing human-like qualities in terms of construction of ideas.

## 7.4 Science Texts

The following analysis is for the four science texts. The 20 most frequently occurring word families (excluding function words) are reported in Table 7.4 in descending order of frequency of occurrence.

**Table 7.4:** Top 20 content words in science texts

| SCI | | | |
|---|---|---|---|
| **Non-GenAI** | **GenAI Scite** | **GenAI Jenni** | **GenAI Yomu** |
| aegypti | fever | fever | fever |
| yfv | yellow | vector | yellow |
| mosquito | transmission | yellow | transmission |
| population | Asia | region | virus |
| Asia | virus | virus | Asia |
| viral | mosquito | Asia | mosquito |
| region | population | Pacific | Pacific |
| transmission | region | risk | risk |
| Pacific | risk | transmission | region |
| vector | ecological | control | potential |
| Africa | potential | area | control |
| saliva | vector | effective | environmental |
| Thailand | human | environmental | human |
| risk | outbreak | population | endemic |
| albopictus | vaccination | factor | measure |
| load | yfv | mosquito | travel |
| particle | aedes | outbreak | vector |
| Taiwan | Pacific | potential | aedes |
| transmit | area | research | breeding |
| virus | climate | strategy | health |

It is evident in the data that all four texts share a degree of similarity in the use of content words, with the following seven words appearing high on the lists: *fever, mosquito, Asia, Pacific, virus, transmission, region.* These words convey the core subject matter suggested in the paper title and GenAI prompt. There are also some differences evident across the four science texts in content word use which appears to reflect the social construction of language, giving the writing human-like qualities in terms of construction of ideas.

# 8. Analysis 4: Low Frequency Word Use

This chapter presents a lexical analysis of low frequency words from the BNC-COCA K5 to K20 word lists appearing in the non-GenAI text and the three GenAI texts, with separate reporting for arts, commerce, law and science. The words in these lists are grouped as word families and are termed *low frequency* to reflect the overall low frequency of occurrence in the combined BNC-COCA corpora. It is expected that this analysis will capture some subject-specific words in the texts assuming a technical nature, although some non-technical words (e.g., proper nouns, genuine low frequency words) may also be included.

## 8.1 Arts Texts

The following analysis is for the four arts texts. The non-GenAI text has been shortened in this analysis to generate a list of words comparable in length to the GenAI texts for ease of comparability.

| Text | Word length (tokens) |
|---|---|
| non-GenAI | 1262 |
| Gen-AI: Scite | 962 |
| Gen-AI: Jenni | 827 |
| Gen-AI: Yomu | 963 |

Table 8.1 presents words appearing in the respective texts from the BNC-COCA K5 to K20 word lists, listed as family groups alphabetically.

**Table 8.1:** Low frequency words in arts texts

| | non-GenAI | GenAI: Scite | GenAI: Jenni | GenAI: Yomu |
|---|---|---|---|---|
| K5-K20 | appropriated | bolster | agonist | advent |
| | conjunction | buffer | dialect | algorithm |
| | deplore | conversely | disposition | amplify |
| | dialectic | drawback | dynamics | appropriated |
| | dichotomy | dynamics | encompass | devalue |
| | disinterested | encompass | foundationalism | dilute |
| | disposition | equate | habitus | disparity |
| | engender | excursion | ingrain | disseminate |
| | formative | expanse | interplay | durable |
| | habitus | extrovert | reap | dynamics |
| | hypocrite | habitus | reciprocity | egalitarian |
| | incite | interplay | socialise | embed |
| | italic | intersect | strata | entrench |
| | lingo | necessitate | stratify | erosion |
| | meme | nuance | tan | foundationalism |
| | microcosm | pandemic | tangible | intellect |
| | mitre | pivot | underscore | interplay |
| | mitt | posit | upbringing | necessitate |
| | pertinent | proactive | | perpetuate |
| | proficient | robust | | reshape |
| | sunder | theorise | | transient |
| | typeset | transactional | | twine |
| | volition | transcend | | ubiquitous |
| | wherein | underscore | | |

It is evident that use of low frequency words is overall numerically less common in the non-GenAI arts text than the GenAI arts texts reflected in the longer length of the non-GenAI text. The data indicate considerable variability in use of words from the BNC-COCA K5 to K20 word lists across the four arts texts with a small degree of commonality. Some words in the list are assuming a technical function in the texts. This includes *habitus* found in the first three listed texts. Overall, the impression is given of human-like variability in low frequency word use in the construction of the four samples of writing.

## 8.2 Commerce Texts

The following analysis is for the four commerce texts. The non-GenAI text has been shortened in this analysis to generate a list of words comparable in length to the GenAI texts for ease of comparability.

| Text | Word length (tokens) |
|---|---|
| non-GenAI | 2843 |
| Gen-AI: Scite | 881 |
| Gen-AI: Jenni | 1075 |
| Gen-AI: Yomu | 1003 |

Table 8.2 presents words appearing in the respective texts from the BNC-COCA K5 to K20 word lists, listed as family groups alphabetically.

**Table 8.2:** Low frequency words in commerce texts

| | non-GenAI | GenAI Scite | GenAI Jenni | GenAI Yomu |
|---|---|---|---|---|
| K5-K20 | appendix | advocacy | alleviate | accrue |
| | caesarean | benchmark | bolster | dynamics |
| | controversy | buffer | depreciate | encompass |
| | differential | catalyst | disentangle | equitable |
| | euro | conducive | disincentive | esteem |
| | exogenous | corroborate | equitable | facet |
| | expire | disparity | ethic | foundationalism |
| | forgo | dynamics | garner | globe |
| | heterogeneous | equitable | hinder | holistic |
| | idiosyncratic | formative | inclusive | intersect |
| | mandatory | foundationalism | maternal | juggle |
| | marital | heighten | multitude | longitudinal |
| | maternal | hinder | necessitate | necessitate |
| | maternity | intersect | neonatal | neurology |
| | maximal | interweave | predicate | nurture |
| | median | longitudinal | retention | pivot |
| | mitigate | maternal | socioeconomic | robust |
| | negligible | nurture | | trajectory |
| | nurture | optimise | | underscore |
| | outlay | precursor | | unravel |
| | outweigh | robust | | |
| | sibling | socioeconomic | | |
| | | trajectory | | |
| | | vaccinate | | |

It is evident that use of low frequency words is overall numerically less common in the non-GenAI commerce text than the GenAI commerce texts reflected in the longer length of the non-GenAI text. The data indicate considerable variability in use of words from the BNC-COCA K5 to K20 word lists across the four commerce texts with a small degree of commonality. Some words in the list are assuming a technical function in the texts. This includes *marital, maternal, nurture* found in more than one of the texts. Overall, the impression is given of human-like variability in low frequency word use in the construction of the four samples of writing.

## 8.3 Law Texts

The following analysis is for the four law texts. The non-GenAI text has been shortened in this analysis to generate a list of words comparable in length to the GenAI texts for ease of comparability.

| Text | Word length (tokens) |
|---|---|
| non-GenAI | 2363 |
| Gen-AI: Scite | 962 |
| Gen-AI: Jenni | 1185 |
| Gen-AI: Yomu | 870 |

Table 8.3 presents words appearing in the respective texts from the BNC-COCA K5 to K20 word lists, listed as family groups alphabetically.

**Table 8.3:** Low frequency words in law texts

| | non-GenAI | GenAI Scite | GenAI Jenni | GenAI Yomu |
|---|---|---|---|---|
| K5-K20 | banister | amplify | acoustic | cohesion |
| | blight | catalyse | biomass | conducive |
| | brow | cohesion | conducive | degrade |
| | censure | cohesive | dynamics | detract |
| | constable | communal | ecology | encompass |
| | cue | conducive | encompass | equitable |
| | detract | contravene | equitable | erode |
| | doe | conversely | facet | facet |
| | emotive | cue | forte | gentrify |
| | eradicate | delinquent | guano | graffiti |
| | flint | devoid | harness | heighten |
| | graffiti | disenfranchise | holistic | inclusive |
| | hamlet | disproportion | interplay | incur |
| | kudos | dynamics | intricate | interplay |
| | laud | empower | intrinsic | intoxicate |
| | locality | encompass | luminous | mitigate |
| | mall | engender | mandatory | necessitate |
| | mannerism | feasible | nurture | perpetuate |

| | non-GenAI | GenAI Scite | GenAI Jenni | GenAI Yomu |
|---|---|---|---|---|
| | penalise | greenery | qualitative | proactive |
| | perpetrate | imperative | relativity | resilience |
| | purport | inclusive | reshape | sensory |
| | reclaim | instil | sonic | strive |
| | regenerate | interplay | tangible | surveillance |
| | renaissance | intoxicate | twine | uphold |
| | revitalise | intricate | underscore | vandal |
| | sanitize | necessitate | vandal | vibrant |
| | sensory | nurture | vegetation | |
| | skate | pivot | | |
| | snob | plaza | | |
| | spiral | posit\proactive | | |
| | stratify | reshape | | |
| | terminology | sensory | | |
| | tolerance | systemic | | |
| | vandal | underline | | |
| | vibrant | underscore | | |
| | vitality | uphold | | |
| | | vandal | | |

It is evident that use of low frequency words is overall numerically less common in the non-GenAI law text than the GenAI law texts reflected in the longer length of the non-GenAI text. The data indicate considerable variability in use of words from the BNC-COCA K5 to K20 word lists across the four law texts with a small degree of commonality. Some words in the list are assuming a technical function in the texts. This includes *habitus* found in the first three listed texts. Overall, the impression is given of human-like variability in low frequency word use in the construction of the four samples of writing.

## 8.4 Science Texts

The following analysis is for the four science texts. The non-GenAI text has been shortened in this analysis to generate a list of words comparable in length to the GenAI texts for ease of comparability.

| Text | Word length (tokens) |
|---|---|
| non-GenAI | 822 |
| Gen-AI: Scite | 736 |
| Gen-AI: Jenni | 798 |
| Gen-AI: Yomu | 891 |

Table 8.4 presents words appearing in the respective texts from the BNC-COCA K5 to K20 word lists, listed as family groups alphabetically.

**Table 8.4:** Low frequency words in science texts

| | non-GenAI | GenAI Scite | GenAI Jenni | GenAI Yomu |
|---|---|---|---|---|
| K5-K20 | accentuate | ascertain | amplify | anthropogenic |
| | basal | biodiversity | archipelago | conducive |
| | dengue | catalyse | converge | deforest |
| | disseminate | conducive | dengue | dynamics |
| | encephalitis | disparity | dynamics | encompass |
| | endemic | dynamics | ecology | endemic |
| | epidemic | ecology | ecosystem | epidemic |
| | epithelial | efficacy | encompass | epidemiology |
| | excrete | elucidate | endemic | equilibrium |
| | genotype | endemic | epidemic | fatigue |
| | gland | epidemic | epidemiology | fortify |
| | incubate | epidemiology | exacerbate | genus |
| | ingest | exacerbate | heighten | humid |
| | insecticide | heighten | incursion | insecticide |
| | mosquito | interplay | insecticide | jaundice |
| | naïve | intricate | interplay | kidney |
| | nausea | mitigate | larva | mitigate |
| | primate | mosquito | mitigate | mosquito |
| | proliferate | paramount | mosquito | nausea |
| | replicate | primate | proactive | necessitate |
| | saliva | proliferate | sanitation | onset |
| | supplant | shear | socioeconomic | primate |
| | susceptible | tacet | surveillance | proactive |
| | uptake | twine | tailor | proliferate |
| | vaccine | vaccinate | vaccinate | requisite |
| | vector | vector | vaccine | reservoir |
| | vertebrate | viral | vector | robust |
| | vicinity | | viral | sanitation |
| | viral | | | sprawl |
| | vomit | | | surveillance |
| | | | | vaccinate |
| | | | | vector |
| | | | | vigil |
| | | | | viral |

It is evident that use of K5 to K20 words is overall similar numerically in the four science texts reflected in the similar length of the texts. While the data indicate some variability in use of words from the BNC-COCA K5 to K20 word lists, overall there is quite a high degree of similarity across the four science texts, evident in the appearance of low frequency words assuming a clearly technical role in the texts, including *mosquito, vaccine, vaccinate, endemic, epidemic, vector.*

# 9. Conclusion

This chapter summarises the key findings from the lexical profiling of the 16 texts in the current study, representing one non-GenAI and three GenAI texts in arts, commerce, law and science.

## 9.1 Use of GSL K1, GSL K2 and AWL Words

The lexical profiling of the four texts in arts, commerce, law and science indicated that:

- All three GenAI arts texts make significantly less use of K1 words, and a corresponding significantly greater use of AWL words, when compared to the non-GenAI arts text.
- All three GenAI commerce texts make significantly less use of K1 words when compared to the non-GenAI commerce text, and a corresponding greater use of AWL words.
- All three GenAI law texts make significantly less use of K1 words, and a corresponding significantly greater use of AWL words, when compared to the non-GenAI law text.
- The lexical profile of the three GenAI science texts displays some greater use of K2 words and also AWL words when compared to the non-GenAI science text.

Following from this, the study revisited the data from Hirsh (2010) analysing four research articles appearing in journals covering arts, economics, law and science (see Table 9.1). This is to provide another point of comparison between the GenAI texts and texts written by humans.

**Table 9.1:** Lexical profile of four academic texts

| Text | Length (tokens) | Lexical coverage (%) | | | |
|---|---|---|---|---|---|
| | | K1 | K2 | AWL | Other words |
| Arts text | 8752 | 68.5 | 5.7 | 11.3 | 14.5 |
| Econ text | 3386 | 70.4 | 4.5 | 10.3 | 14.7 |
| Law text | 12726 | 80.8 | 4.5 | 6.4 | 8.3 |
| Sci text | 2305 | 70.0 | 5.2 | 9.7 | 15.1 |

In comparing the three GenAI texts in arts, commerce, law and science with these four non-GenAI journal articles, the following findings emerged:

- The three AI-generated arts texts are making significantly greater use of academic words and correspondingly less use of the first thousand high frequency words than is the case with the four non-GenAI published research articles.
- The three AI-generated commerce texts are making significantly greater use of academic words and a pattern across the three texts of less use of the first thousand high frequency words than is the case with the four non-GenAI published research articles.
- The three AI-generated law texts are making significantly greater use of academic words and correspondingly less use of the first thousand high frequency words than is the case with the four non-GenAI published research articles.
- The three AI-generated science texts are making significantly greater use of K2 words and academic words and correspondingly less use of the first thousand high frequency words than is the case with the four non-GenAI published research articles.

The central finding emerging from this analysis is that there is a pattern across the AI-generated texts, which are shorter than the human (non-GenAI) texts, of less use of the first thousand words of English, and correspondingly greater use of academic words. It is outside the scope of the current study to investigate the impact of this pattern on the suitability of the texts as reading material in university settings. This is an area for future research to investigate.

## 9.2 Use of BNC-COCA K1 to K10 Words

The lexical profiling of the four texts in arts, commerce, law and science in terms of use of BNC-COCA K1 to K10 indicated that:

- The three GenAI arts texts make less use of K1 words than the non-GenAI arts text and, correspondingly, make greater use of K2 and K3 words than is the case with the non-GenAI text.
- The three GenAI commerce texts make slightly less use of K1 words than the non-GenAI commerce text and, correspondingly, make slightly greater use of K2 words than is the case with the non-GenAI text.
- The three GenAI law texts make considerably less use of K1 words than the non-GenAI law text and, correspondingly, make considerably greater use of K2 and K3 words than is the case with the non-GenAI text.
- The three GenAI science texts make less use of K1 words than the non-GenAI science text and, correspondingly, make slightly greater use of K2 and K3 words than is the case with the non-GenAI text.

The central finding emerging from this analysis is that there is a pattern across the AI-generated texts, which are shorter than the human (non-GenAI) texts, of less use of the most frequently occurring thousand words (K1) of the BNC-COCA combined corpora, and correspondingly greater use of the second most frequently occurring thousand words (K2) and to some extent also greater use of the third most frequently occurring thousand words (K3). This finding is in line with the finding in Section 9.1. Thus, as with the finding in Section 9.1, it is outside the scope of the current study to investigate the impact of this pattern on the suitability of the texts as reading material in university settings. This is an area for future research to investigate.

## 9.3 20 Most Frequently Occurring Content Words

The lexical profiling for the four texts in arts, commerce, law and science to identify the 20 most frequently occurring content words (i.e., excluding function words) indicated the following:

- a degree of similarity in the use of content words for all four arts texts, representative of a core technical vocabulary for the topic area
- a degree of similarity in the use of content words for all four commerce texts, representative of a core technical vocabulary for the topic area
- a degree of similarity in the use of content words for all four law texts, representative of a core technical vocabulary for the topic area
- a degree of similarity in the use of content words for all four science texts, representative of a core technical vocabulary for the topic area

In summary, for arts, commerce, law and science, the following general findings emerge:

- All four texts share a degree of similarity, generally high, in the use of content words, with a selection of common words appearing high on the lists for all four texts.
- These words convey the core subject matter and thus can be regarded as technical (subject specific) vocabulary.
- There are also some differences evident across the texts in content word use which appears to reflect the social construction of language, giving the writing human-like qualities in terms of construction of ideas.

The central finding emerging from this analysis is that there is a pattern across the AI-generated texts, which are shorter than the human (non-GenAI) texts, of similar use of words associated with central subject matter, reflected in similar words in the four texts appearing among the 20 most frequently occurring content words. This suggests that the AI-generated writing investigated in the current study shares a degree of similar technicality in word use with a human written journal article on the same topic.

## 9.4 Use of Low Frequency Words

Lexical analysis was conducted to identify low frequency words from the BNC-COCA K5 to K20 word lists appearing in the non-GenAI text and the three GenAI texts, with separate reporting for arts, commerce, law and science. The words in these lists are grouped as word families and are termed *low frequency* to reflect the overall low frequency of occurrence in the combined BNC-COCA corpora. It is expected that this analysis will capture some subject-specific words in the texts assuming a technical nature, although non-technical words (e.g., proper nouns and genuine low frequency words) may be included. The key findings were:

- use of low frequency words is overall numerically less common in the non-GenAI arts text than the GenAI texts; considerable variability in use of words from the BNC-COCA K5 to K20 word lists is evident across the four arts texts and there is a small degree of commonality across the texts in the form of technical words reflective of the subject matter.
- use of low frequency words is overall numerically less common in the non-GenAI commerce text than the GenAI texts; considerable variability in use of words from the BNC-COCA K5 to K20 word lists is evident across the four

commerce texts and there is some commonality across the texts in the form of technical words reflective of the subject matter.
- use of low frequency words is overall numerically less common in the non-GenAI law text than the GenAI texts; considerable variability in use of words from the BNC-COCA K5 to K20 word lists is evident across the four law texts and there is a small degree of commonality in the form of technical words across the texts reflective of the subject matter.
- use of low frequency words is numerically similar across the four science texts; some variability in use of words from the BNC-COCA K5 to K20 word lists is evident across the four science texts and there is quite a high degree of commonality in the form of technical words across the texts reflective of the subject matter.

To sum up for the four subject areas:

- Numerically, there is higher use of low frequency words in the GenAI texts than in the non-GenAI texts in arts, commerce and law, whereas there is similar numerical use of these words across the four science texts.
- There is considerable variability in use of words from the BNC-COCA K5 to K20 word lists across the texts in arts, commerce, law and science.
- There is some commonality in the form of low frequency words assuming a technical word role across texts in arts, commerce and law, with this pattern most apparent in science where technical words from the BNC-COCA K5 to K10 word list are most widely used, reflective of the subject matter being discussed in the writing samples analysed.

The central finding emerging from this analysis is that there is a pattern across the AI-generated texts, which are shorter than the human (non-GenAI) texts, of proportionately more use of low frequency words than the human written (non-GenAI) equivalent papers in arts, commerce and law, but not science. The current study has not explored this feature of the GenAI texts in more detail, but it does warrant future investigation to appreciate the nature of AI-generated written discourse in university settings.

## 9.5 Final Comments

Recent technological advancements in GenAI have ushered in the availability and use in universities of Large Language Models (LLM), symbolised by the public availability of *ChatGPT* and *DeepSeek*, as well as an evergrowing number of GenAI tools, all built on Machine Learning (ML) and Natural Language Processing (NLP). These GenAI tools are capable of generating text in response to written prompts, with some indications that these GenAI responses can be viewed as acceptable alternatives to human-generated texts (see Chapter 2). The hopes of AI to be able to perform tasks typically requiring human intelligence are being realised in numerous contexts, including academic settings. Yet, there are concerns being raised which are important to be addressed, as documented in Chapter 2, regarding:

- the capacity of GenAI to provide satisfactory responses to more cognitively demanding tasks
- the possibility of oversimplification or misrepresentation of complex research areas by GenAI
- the capacity of GenAI to appropriately negotiate sensitive or controversial subject matter

In terms of university responses to the technology, the focus has taken the form of revised and new policies, guidelines and resources reflecting two broad approaches, as discussed in Chapter 2:

- Pedagogical applications: designed to promote effective incorporation of GenAI into teaching and learning programs, reflective of university values and visions about the nature of learning
- Prevention strategies: designed to discourage and identify inappropriate use of GenAI, particularly in relation to submitted assessment tasks

At another level, some universities have adopted text checking programs developed to identify possible inclusion of GenAI content within a text. Use of such text checking programs is intended to discourage students from making unethical use of GenAI content within their writing and identify possible cases for follow-up investigation. Concerns raised about use of such GenAI detecting tools, as documented in Chapter 2, relate to:

- the potential for stifling pedagogically-sound use of GenAI, whereby students may be deterred from experimental use of GenAI in the planning for their writing in the fear that such use may expose them to malpractice accusations;
- the potential for false positives;

- the challenge of verifying detection results, leading to possible lengthy and stressful investigations of student writing processes by academic institutions, inducing severe anxiety for affected students.

With future iterations of Large Language Models (LLM), and increased interest in the use of AI-generated writing for various learning purposes in academic settings, it is expected that the GenAI tools made available will be scrutinised at multiple levels to assess their suitability for generating texts used for background reading and research purposes by students and researchers. Such scrutiny will need to build on the current study's investigation of vocabulary use, to explore human interactions with the technology, to better understand how Generative AI is shaping or reshaping language use and learning behaviour in tertiary settings.

# References


Aishwarya, S. / Selvamurugan, C. / Parthiban, K. G. / Nathan, B. / Prabhakar, J. Manoj / Noordeen, A. Mohamed 2024. Generative AI in Focus: A Comprehensive Review of Leading Models Across Modalities. In *2024 4th International Conference on Ubiquitous Computing and Intelligent Information Systems (ICUIS)*, IEEE, 1–9.

Al-Amin, Md / Ali, Mohammad Shazed / Salam, Abdus / Khan, Arif / Ali, Ashraf / Ullah, Ahsan / Alam, Md Nur / Chowdhury, Shamsul Kabir 2024. History of Generative Artificial Intelligence (AI) Chatbots: Past, Present, and Future Development. *ArXiv preprint.* 2402, 05122.

AlAfnan, Mohammad Awad 2025. Large Language Models as Computational Linguistics Tools: A Comparative Analysis of ChatGPT and Google Machine Translations. *Journal of Artificial Intelligence and Technology.* 5, 20–32.

Alemanno, Francesco / Aquaro, Miriam / Kanter, Ido / Barra, Adriano / Agliari, Elena 2023. Supervised Hebbian Learning. *Europhysics Letters* 141/1, 11001.

Ardito, Cesare Giulio 2024. Generative AI Detection in Higher Education Assessments. *New Directions for Teaching and Learning,* advance view.

Bandyopadhyay, Dibyanayan / Bhattacharjee, Soham / Ekbal, Asif 2025. Thinking Machines: A Survey of LLM Based Reasoning Strategies. *ArXiv preprint.* 2503, 10814.

Banh, Leonardo / Strobel, Gero 2023. Generative Artificial Intelligence. *Electronic Markets.* 33/1, 63.

Bauer, Laurie / Nation, Paul 1993. Word Families. *International Journal of Lexicography.* 6/4, 253–279.

Belkina, Marina / Daniel, Scott / Sasha Nikolic, Sasha / Haque, Rezwanul / Lyden, Sarah / Neal, Peter / Grundy, Sarah / Hassan, Ghulam M. 2025. Implementing Generative AI (GenAI) in Higher Education: A Systematic Review of Case Studies. *Computers and Education: Artificial Intelligence*. 100407.

Benko, Attila / Lányi, Cecília Sik 2009. History of Artificial Intelligence. In *Encyclopedia of Information Science and Technology*. IGI Global, 1759–1762.

Bittle, Kyle / El-Gayar, Omar 2025. Generative AI and Academic Integrity in Higher Education: A Systematic Review and Research Agenda. *Information*. 16/4, 296.

Campion, Mary E. / Elley, Warwick B. 1971. *An Academic Vocabulary List*. Wellington: New Zealand Council of Educational Research.

Chang, Yupeng / Wang, Xu / Wang, Jindong / Wu, Yuan / Yang, Linyi / Zhu, Kaijie / Chen, Hao et al. 2024. A Survey on Evaluation of Large Language Models. *ACM Transactions on Intelligent Systems and Technology*. 15/3, 1–45.

Cobb, Tom 2025. *Compleat Lexical Tutor*. Accessed 26 April 2025. <www.lextutor.ca/vp/comp>.

Coxhead, Averil 1998. *An Academic Word List* (English Language Institute Occasional Publication No. 18). Wellington: Victoria University of Wellington.

Coxhead, Averil 2000. A New Academic Word List. *TESOL Quarterly*. 34/2, 213–238.

Coxhead, Averil / Hirsh, David 2007. A Pilot Science-Specific Word List. *Revue Francaise de Linguistique Appliquee*. 12/2, 65–78.

Davies, Mark 2009. The 385+ Million Word Corpus of Contemporary American English (1990–2008+): Design, Architecture, and Linguistic Insights. *International Journal of Corpus Linguistics*. 14/2, 159–190.

Dixon, Steve 2004. A Brief History of Robots and Automata. *TDR: The Drama Review*. 48/4, 16–25.

Eberhard, David M. / Simons, Gary F. / Fennig, Charles D. (eds) 2025. *Ethnologue: Languages of the World* (28th edition). Dallas, TX: SIL International. <http://www.ethnologue.com>

Elley, Warwick B. / Reid, Neil A. 1969. *Progressive Achievement Tests of Reading Comprehension and Reading Vocabulary*. Wellington: New Zealand Council for Educational Research.

Francis, Nigel J. / Jones, Sue / Smith, David P. 2025. Generative AI in Higher Education: Balancing Innovation and Integrity. *British Journal of Biomedical Science*. 81, 14048.

Ghadessy, Mohsen 1979. Frequency Counts, Word Lists, and Material Preparation: A New Approach. *English Teaching Forum.* 17/1, 24–27.

Goulden, Robin / Nation, Paul / Read, John 1990. How Large Can a Receptive Vocabulary Be? *Applied Linguistics* 11/4, 341–363.

Grzybowski, Andrzej / Pawlikowska–Łagód, Katarzyna / Lambert, W. Clark 2024. A History of Artificial Intelligence. *Clinics in Dermatology.* 42/3, 221–229.

Hanafi, Ahmed M. / Al-mansi, Mohamed M. / Al-Sharif, Omar A. 2025. Generative AI in Academia: A Comprehensive Review of Applications and Implications for the Research Process. *International Journal of Engineering and Applied Sciences.* 2/1, 91–110.

Hirsh, David / Nation, Paul 1992. What Vocabulary Size Is Needed to Read Unsimplified Texts for Pleasure? *Reading in a Foreign Language.* 8, 689–696.

Ho, Anson / Besiroglu, Tamay / Erdil, Ege / Owen, David / Rahman, Robi / Guo, Zifan C. / Atkinson, David / Thompson, Neil / Sevilla, Jaime 2024. Algorithmic Progress in Language Models. *Advances in Neural Information Processing Systems.* 37, 58245–58283.

Hounshell, David 1997. The Cold War, RAND, and the Generation of Knowledge, 1946–1962. *Historical Studies in the Physical and Biological Sciences.* 27/2, 237–267.

Hwang, Kyongho / Nation, Paul. 1989. Reducing the Vocabulary Load and Encouraging Vocabulary Learning through Reading Newspapers. *Reading in a Foreign Language.* 6, 323–335.

Jin, Yueqiao / Ya, Lixiang / Echeverria, Vanessa / Gašević, Dragan / Martinez-Maldonado, Roberto 2025. Generative AI in Higher Education: A Global Perspective of Institutional Adoption Policies and Guidelines. *Computers and Education: Artificial Intelligence.* 8, 100348.

Khanuja, Simran / Bansal, Diksha / Mehtani, Sarvesh / Khosla, Savya / Dey, Atreyee / Gopalan, Balaji / Margam, Dilip Kumar et al. 2021. Muril: Multilingual Representations for Indian Languages. *ArXiv preprint. 2103, 10730.*

Khlaif, Zuheir N. / Alkouk, Wejdan Awadallah / Salama, Nisreen / Abu Eideh, Belal 2025. Redesigning Assessments for AI-Enhanced Learning: A Framework for Educators in the Generative AI Era. *Education Sciences.* 15/2, 174.

Kim, Jinhee / Yu, Seongryeong / Detrick, Rita / Li, Na 2025. Exploring Students' Perspectives on Generative AI-assisted Academic Writing. *Education and Information Technologies.* 30/1, 1265–1300.

Kühl, Niklas / Schemmer, Max / Goutier, Marc / Satzger, Gerhard 2022. Artificial Intelligence and Machine Learning. *Electronic Markets.* 32/4, 2235–2244.

Lee, Raymond 2025. Large Language Models (LLMs) and Generative Artificial Intelligence (GenAI). *Natural Language Processing: A Textbook with Python Implementation*. Singapore: Springer Nature Singapore, 241–273.

Leech, Geoffrey / Rayson, Paul 2014. *Word Frequencies in Written and Spoken English: Based on the British National Corpus*. London: Routledge.

Liu, Fei / Tong, Xialiang / Yuan, Mingxuan / Zhang, Qingfu 2023. Algorithm Evolution using Large Language Model. *ArXiv preprint. 2311, 15249.*

Liu, Yang / Cao, Jiahuan / Liu, Chongyu / Ding, Kai / Jin, Lianwen 2024. Datasets for Large Language Models: A Comprehensive Survey. *ArXiv preprint. 2402, 18041.*

Luo, Jiahui 2024. A Critical Review of GenAI Policies in Higher Education Assessment: A Call to Reconsider the "Originality" of Students' Work. *Assessment & Evaluation in Higher Education.* 49/5, 651–664.

Lynn, Robert W. 1973. Preparing Word Lists: A Suggested Method. *RELC Journal.* 4/1, 25–32.

Matsuoka, Warren / Hirsh, David 2010. Vocabulary Learning through Reading: Does an ELT Course Book Provide Good Opportunities? *Reading in a Foreign Language.* 22/1, 56–70.

Matsuoka, Warren / Hirsh, David 2018. The Specialised Vocabulary of High School Science. In Hirsh, David (ed.) *Explorations in Second Language Vocabulary Research*. Bern: Peter Lang, 55–99.

McDonald, Nora / Johri, Aditya / Ali, Areej / Collier, Aayushi Hingle 2025. Generative Artificial Intelligence in Higher Education: Evidence from an Analysis of Institutional Policies and Guidelines. *Computers in Human Behavior: Artificial Humans*. 100121.

Nation, Paul 2025. *Vocabulary Lists*. <www.wgtn.ac.nz/lals/resources/paul-nations-resources/vocabulary-lists>

Nation, Paul / Hwang, Kyongho 1995. Where Would General Service Vocabulary Stop and Special Purposes Begin? *System.* 23/1, 35–41.

Ogunleye, Bayode / Zakariyyah, Kudirat Ibilola / Ajao, Oluwaseun / Olayinka, Olakunle / Sharma, Hemlata 2024. Higher Education Assessment Practice in the Era of Generative AI Tools. *ArXiv preprint. 2404, 01036.*

Oliveira, Arlindo L. / Figueiredo, Mário A.T. 2024. Artificial Intelligence: Historical Context and State of the Art. *Multidisciplinary Perspectives on Artificial Intelligence and the Law.* 3.

Ostendorff, Malte / Suarez, Pedro Ortiz / Lage, Lucas Fonseca / Rehm, Georg 2024. LLM-Datasets: An Open Framework for Pretraining Datasets of Large Language Models. In *First Conference on Language Modeling.* Philadelphia, PA.

Phillips-Wren, Gloria / Virvou, Maria 2025. Issues and Trends in Generative AI Technologies for Decision Making. *Intelligent Decision Technologies.* 18724981251320551.

Praninskas, Jean 1972. *American University Word List.* London: Longman.

Prather, James / Leinonen, Juho / Kiesler, Natalie / Benario, Jamie Gorson / Lau, Sam / MacNeil, Stephen / Norouzi, Narges et al. 2025. Beyond the Hype: A Comprehensive Review of Current Trends in Generative AI Research, Teaching Practices, and Tools. *2024 Working Group Reports on Innovation and Technology in Computer Science Education,* 300–338.

Sapkota, Ranjan / Raza, Shaina / Karkee, Manoj 2025. Comprehensive Analysis of Transparency and Accessibility of ChatGPT, DeepSeek, and other SoTA Large Language Models. *ArXiv preprint. 2502, 18505.*

Scassellati, Brian 2025. MIT Cog. *Humanoid Robotics: A Reference*, 91–100.

Sousa, Ana Elisa / Paula Cardoso. Use of Generative AI by Higher Education Students 2025. *Electronics.* 14/7, 1258.

van Stein, Niki / Kononova, Anna V. / Kotthoff, Lars / Bäck, Thomas 2025. Code Evolution Graphs: Understanding Large Language Model Driven Design of Algorithms. *ArXiv preprint. 2503, 16668.*

Wang, Hui / Dang, Anh / Wu, Zihao / Mac, Son 2024. Generative AI in Higher Education: Seeing ChatGPT through Universities' Policies, Resources, and Guidelines. *Computers and Education: Artificial Intelligence.* 7, 100326.

Wang, Zichong / Chu, Zhibo / Doan, Thang Viet / Ni, Shiwen / Yang, Min / Zhang, Wenbin 2024. History, Development, and Principles of Large Language Models: An Introductory Survey. *AI and Ethics,* 1–17.

West, Michael 1953. *A General Service List of English Words*. London: Longman, Green & Co.

Xi, Zhiheng / Chen, Wenxiang / Guo, Xin / He, Wei / Ding, Yiwen / Hong, Boyang / Zhang, Ming et al. 2025. The Rise and Potential of Large Language Model Based Agents: A Survey. *Science China Information Sciences.* 68/2, 121101.

Xu, Qiming / Feng, Zheng / Gong, Chenwei / Wu, Xubo / Zhao, Haopeng / Ye, Zhi / Li, Zichao / Wei, Changsong 2024. Applications of Explainable AI in Natural Language Processing. *Global Academic Frontiers.* 2/3, 51–64.

Xue, Guo-Yi / Nation, Paul 1984. A University Word List. *Language Learning and Communication.* 3/2, 215–229.

Yu, Yijiong / Dai, Ziyun / Wang, Zekun / Wang, Wei / Chen, Ran / Pei, Ji 2025. OpenCSG Chinese Corpus: A Series of High-quality Chinese Datasets for LLM Training. *ArXiv preprint. 2501, 08197.*

# Appendix 1. Arts Text GenAI Scite

## Bourdieu, Social Capital and Online Interaction

The interplay between Bourdieu's concept of social capital and online interactions has become increasingly significant in understanding how digital platforms shape social relationships and community dynamics. Bourdieu theorized social capital as the resources and benefits individuals derive from their social networks, emphasizing the importance of social ties in achieving personal and collective goals. This framework can be extended to explore how online interactions contribute to the formation and maintenance of various types of social capital.

To comprehend the nuances of social capital in online settings, one must differentiate between bonding and bridging social capital, as articulated by Williams Williams (2006). Bonding social capital refers to the ties among individuals who share similar backgrounds, promoting strong, supportive connections. In contrast, bridging social capital encompasses relationships that connect diverse social groups, potentially leading to broader networking opportunities and access to varying resources. Online platforms, such as social media and forums, are critical in facilitating both types of social capital through digital interactions.

Studies indicate that active participation in online communities promotes the cultivation of social capital. For instance, Weiqin et al. found that extraverted individuals who actively seek information and engage in communication on platforms like Facebook experience greater social capital than those who passively consume content (Weiqin et al., 2016). These findings emphasize the importance of proactive engagement over passive consumption in building social networks. The active pursuit of interactions strengthens existing relationships and fosters connections with new individuals, enhancing bridging social capital.

The importance of online social capital has been particularly highlighted in recent studies during the COVID-19 pandemic. Research by Fahy and Barry illustrates that online social capital can bolster well-being, particularly for individuals experiencing loneliness during lockdowns. Their findings suggest that computer-mediated communication offers a critical means for forming and maintaining social connections that may otherwise be absent due to physical distancing (Fahy & Barry, 2024). This situation reinforces Bourdieu's assertion that social capital can act as a buffer during periods of isolation, allowing individuals to derive emotional and practical support from their connections.

Moreover, the transition from online interactions to offline relationships demonstrates the transformative potential of digital spaces. Shen and Cage describe how meetups based on online communities can convert virtual connections into meaningful, face-to-face relationships, thereby enhancing both bonding and bridging social capital (Shen & Cage, 2013). Their research shows that these excursions into the real world help solidify social ties that began in the online realm, validating the role of online platforms in fostering genuine community participation.

The communicative strategies utilized within online networks also play a pivotal role in shaping social capital. Ellison et al. investigate how specific communication practices on Facebook influence the perceived social capital levels among university students. Their findings suggest that different strategies yield varying degrees of social capital benefits, underscoring the need for individuals to navigate their online interactions strategically to maximize relational outcomes (Ellison et al., 2011). This insight aligns with Bourdieu's emphasis on the relational context of social capital, where the nature of interconnections fundamentally affects the resources available to individuals.

Additionally, the operational mechanics of online communities have demonstrated favorable impacts on maintaining social ties and enhancing social capital. Lee and Lee argue that computer-mediated communication networks help bridge geographical gaps, facilitating social interactions that might not be possible otherwise (Lee & Lee, 2010). This capability is essential in a globalized world where people seek diverse perspectives and opportunities from varied social groups. The ability of online platforms to transcend physical boundaries serves to strengthen both bonding and bridging capital in unique and meaningful ways.

Conversely, it is crucial to recognize potential drawbacks in the realm of online social capital. Some studies suggest that the quality of online interactions may not equate to the richness of offline relationships, leading to a perception of social isolation despite frequent digital engagements. Tushya et al. found no significant relationship between online social capital and offline social capital for members of online gaming communities, indicating that merely contributing to virtual social spaces does not inherently foster real-world connections (Tushya et al., 2023).

This gap emphasizes that while online interactions can expand social networks, they do not automatically translate into meaningful offline relationships.

Furthermore, the nuances of cultural capital and social capital manifest distinctly in online interactions. Lin and Chen explore how online tagging behaviors are influenced by both cultural and social capital, indicating that users with different capital profiles engage with online content differently, which in turn affects overall community dynamics (Lin & Chen, 2012). This intersection posits that online interactions are not merely transactional but are deeply rooted in the social and cultural backgrounds of users.

Bourdieu's concept of habitus also provides a lens through which to analyze online interactions. Costa's work emphasizes that the digital practices of scholars are influenced by their existing social capital, underscoring the interplay between personal experience and online engagement practices (Costa, 2014). Consequently, scholars with robust social networks may thrive in online environments by sharing knowledge and resources, which inherently cultivates further social capital.

In synthesizing these insights, it becomes clear that online interactions significantly influence social capital's formation and evolution. They serve as both mechanisms for reinforcing existing social ties and platforms for creating new connections that broaden social horizons. Understanding the dynamics of social capital in the digital age requires integrating Bourdieu's theoretical framework with contemporary studies of online behavior.

In conclusion, Bourdieu's concepts of social capital and habitus provide a robust framework for analyzing online interactions and their implications for social connectivity. The positive aspects of online engagement, particularly in fostering diverse and expansive social networks, reveal the transformative potential of digital communication. However, challenges remain regarding the depth and quality of these connections, necessitating ongoing research into how individuals navigate their social capital in increasingly digital spaces.

Source: Scite for Research (generated 25/04/2025)

# Appendix 2. Arts Text GenAI Jenni

## Bourdieu, Social Capital and Online Interaction

The exploration of Pierre Bourdieu's concepts of capital, field, and habitus within the context of online interactions reveals a complex interplay of power dynamics and social stratification in the digital realm. Bourdieu's theoretical framework, emphasizing the dialectical relationship between social structures and individual agency, offers a lens through which to examine how online platforms function as spaces where social capital is accumulated, exchanged, and leveraged (Souza & Silvino, 2018). Understanding Bourdieu's key concepts, such as habitus, practice, field, and the various forms of capital (cultural, economic, social, and symbolic), is crucial for analyzing the dynamics of online social interactions (Power, 1999). Capital, in Bourdieu's view, encompasses not only economic resources but also cultural and social assets that individuals accumulate and utilize to gain advantages in various social fields (Ignatow & Robinson, 2017). Cultural capital refers to the knowledge, skills, education, and tastes that individuals acquire through their upbringing and socialization, influencing their ability to navigate and succeed in specific fields (Huang, 2019). Habitus, on the other hand, embodies the ingrained dispositions, perceptions, and practices that individuals develop as a result of their social experiences, shaping their actions and interactions within social fields (Huang, 2019). The concept of field represents the social arena in which individuals compete for resources and recognition, with each field having its own set of rules, norms, and power structures that influence the strategies and outcomes of those involved (Tan & Liu, 2022).

Bourdieu's concepts of habitus and field provide a valuable framework for understanding how individuals navigate the social world, integrating insights from various sociological perspectives (Eisenberg, 2007). Bourdieu's work highlights how cultural capital is gained through initial learning and is unconsciously influenced by the surroundings (Webb et al., 2002). Within the realm of online interactions, these concepts become particularly relevant as individuals engage in digital fields characterized by unique norms, hierarchies, and forms of capital (Shammas & Sandberg, 2015). Social capital, defined as the network of relationships and connections that individuals can mobilize for their benefit, plays a significant role in shaping online experiences and outcomes. Online platforms, with their capacity to connect individuals across geographical boundaries and social strata, provide opportunities for expanding social networks and accumulating social capital (Cheng, 2023; Webb et al., 2002). However, the distribution of social capital in online spaces is often uneven, reflecting existing inequalities in the offline world. Bourdieu's work underscores the agonistic nature of social relations and the role of domination, emphasizing the contextual factors that shape social phenomena and the transformative effects of sustained engagement within specific domains of social action (Shammas & Sandberg, 2015).

The dynamics of online interaction are significantly shaped by the interplay of cultural capital, social capital, and the specific characteristics of the online field. Individuals with high levels of cultural capital, such as those with strong digital literacy skills or a deep understanding of online culture, may be better positioned to leverage online platforms for their benefit. Moreover, individuals with extensive social networks can draw upon their connections to access information, opportunities, and support within online communities. However, the conversion of social capital into tangible benefits in the online realm is not always straightforward, as factors such as trust, reciprocity, and the specific norms of the online community can influence the outcomes of social interactions (Gómez, 2020). The affordances of social network sites significantly shape communication processes and social capital outcomes, emphasizing the role of profiles, articulated networks, and content streams in facilitating social capital exchanges (Ellison & Vitak, 2015). The digital landscape has been linked to both increases and decreases in social capital, presenting a dualistic perspective on its impact (Phulari et al., 2010). The formation of social capital in online social networks involves the ability to access resources from network members, including information, relationships, and organizational capabilities (Phulari et al., 2010).

The concept of digital capital emerges as a crucial element in understanding the dynamics of online interactions, encompassing the technical skills, knowledge, and social connections that individuals leverage to navigate and succeed in digital environments. Digital capital, encompassing technical skills, access, and online networks, has become increasingly important in contemporary society (McGillivray & Mahon, 2021). The third-level digital divide highlights the unequal ability of individuals to convert economic, cultural, and social capital into digital capital and to reap the benefits of online engagement. Economic capital serves as the foundational layer of digital inequality, creating tangible obstacles to access, while cultural capital is transformed into digital capital through techno-socialization, and social capital is converted through social practices and support (Gómez, 2020). The ongoing digital transformation has significantly impacted public relations, highlighting the importance of understanding and measuring digital capital in various contexts (Bannykh & Kostina, 2022). Individuals transform digital resources into social resources through online interactions, exploiting the advantages offered by the internet.

Online platforms offer unique opportunities for individuals to connect with others who share similar interests, experiences, or health conditions, potentially leading to the formation of valuable social connections and the accumulation of social medical capital (Panzarasa et al., 2020).

Source: Jenni (generated 25/04/2025)

# Appendix 3. Arts Text GenAI Yomu

## Bourdieu, Social Capital and Online Interaction

### Introduction to Bourdieu's Social Capital

Bourdieu's theory of social capital is a crucial component of his broader theoretical framework, which includes economic, cultural, and symbolic capital. Bourdieu defines social capital as the actual or potential resources linked to a durable network of institutionalized relationships of mutual acquaintance and recognition. This form of capital is significant because it captures the value embedded in social networks, emphasizing the role of relationships in generating economic and cultural benefits for individuals and groups.

The relevance of social capital lies in its ability to facilitate coordinated actions and meaningful connections. Social networks, according to Bourdieu, provide their members with collectively owned capital, which they can leverage to access information, influence, and opportunities. The interconnectedness within a social network allows individuals to leverage these resources to their advantage, thus becoming an essential aspect of both personal and group success.

In the contemporary context, where digital and online interactions have become ubiquitous, Bourdieu's concept offers an insightful lens through which to analyze the dynamics and implications of online social networks. These networks often mirror traditional social structures and hierarchies, offering platforms for both the creation and erosion of social capital. Understanding this connection is crucial for grasping the modern implications of Bourdieu's theory.

### Online Interaction as a Form of Network

Online interactions fundamentally reshape traditional social networks. With the advent of digital communication technologies, online platforms such as social media, forums, and professional networking sites have emerged as dominant spaces for social interaction. These platforms extend Bourdieu's concept of social capital by recreating traditional networks within a virtual space, allowing for global connectivity beyond geographical boundaries.

Social capital in online interactions manifests through various forms: individuals can build professional networks on sites like LinkedIn, maintain personal relationships through Facebook, or engage in community discussions on Reddit. These interactions contribute to the formation of durable networks that reflect Bourdieu's notion of social capital, providing access to information, resources, and opportunities previously unavailable in more confined social circles.

However, digital interactions pose unique challenges. While they democratize access to networks, they also introduce complexities regarding the authenticity and depth of connections. Online, the quality of relationships can be varied, with some ties being superficial or transient, contrasting with the 'institutionalized' nature of relationships Bourdieu describes. Hence, the stability and reliability of social capital built online may differ from that developed through face-to-face interactions.

## Impact on Social Structures

Bourdieu's exploration of social capital acknowledges the perpetuation of social inequalities through social networks. Online interactions can both challenge and reinforce traditional social structures. On one hand, they democratize access to networks and knowledge, potentially leveling the playing field for individuals who historically lacked access to certain social circles.

On the other hand, online platforms can also entrench existing hierarchies. Social media algorithms often favor content and connections that replicate a user's existing network, perpetuating echo chambers. This can lead to increased segregation and polarization, reflecting and even amplifying real-world inequities. The ability of individuals to effectively manage and leverage their online social capital thus becomes critical in navigating these digital landscapes.

Furthermore, the digital divide still exists, limiting access to the internet for some populations and creating new forms of exclusion. Those lacking digital literacy or resources to engage online are at a disadvantage, unable to fully participate in the social capital available within virtual networks. This disparity highlights the necessity of addressing access issues to truly harness the democratizing potential of online interactions.

## The Role of Social Media in Cultural Capital

Social media platforms serve as critical arenas for the development and exchange of cultural capital, a concept intertwined with social capital. Bourdieu argues that cultural capital consists of non-financial social assets, such as education, intellect, and style of speech, that promote social mobility. In an online context, social media serves as a space where cultural capital can be both displayed and challenged.

Individuals often showcase their cultural knowledge and skills on social media through the sharing of content that reflects personal tastes, values, and skills. This digital expression contributes to one's online identity and status, allowing others to recognize and validate their cultural capital. Unlike traditional settings where cultural capital is restricted to specific social classes, the online sphere allows for broader expression and recognition.

However, social media also complicates the maintenance and transmission of cultural capital. The rapid pace of content creation and dissemination challenges the stability of cultural symbols and norms. The risk of cultural appropriation and the devaluation or dilution of cultural capital online necessitate ongoing negotiation and adaptation by users. Thus, the interaction between social and cultural capital in online settings provides both opportunities and challenges for individuals seeking to navigate this space effectively.

## Conclusion: Implications of Bourdieu's Theory in the Digital Era

Bourdieu's concept of social capital remains profoundly relevant in exploring the dynamics of online interactions. As digital platforms become central to social life, they transform how individuals build and leverage social networks, offering new opportunities and challenges. These platforms provide the potential to create more egalitarian networks that can bridge traditional social divides, while simultaneously risking the perpetuation of existing inequalities.

The ongoing evolution of digital interactions calls for a nuanced understanding of how social capital functions in this new landscape. While Bourdieu's framework offers foundational insights, the complexities of online network dynamics require adaptation and further investigation. The implications for social research and policy must consider how to maximize the benefits of online interactions while addressing the emerging challenges and inequalities.

Ultimately, Bourdieu's theory offers a critical lens for understanding the modern social world. By acknowledging the interplay between social, cultural, and economic capital in online contexts, we gain valuable insights into the potential for digital platforms to reshape social structures and influence individual success in an increasingly interconnected world.

Source: Yomu (generated 26/04/2025)

# Appendix 4. Commerce Text GenAI Scite

## Paid parental leave and children's schooling outcomes

The connection between paid parental leave and children's educational outcomes is a topic of increasing relevance, particularly as research identifies the broader social and health benefits of such policies. The significance of paid parental leave extends beyond immediate parental recovery; it fundamentally impacts children's long-term educational and developmental outcomes.

Several studies have established a correlation between paid parental leave and enhanced child well-being. Specifically, longer paid leave periods contribute to better child health, which is often a precursor to improved educational performance (Puliyel et al., 2021), (Nandi et al., 2016). For instance, a systematic review conducted by Nandi et al. highlights that the availability of paid parental leave is positively associated with lower rates of infant mortality and better overall health metrics for children, which can facilitate their educational success (Nandi et al., 2016). Moreover, the stability provided by parental leave allows parents to invest quality time in their children's early developmental stages, leading to cognitive and emotional benefits that subsequently manifest in academic settings (Burtle & Bezruchka, 2016).

The intersection of paid parental leave and educational outcomes also reflects differences in social contexts and economic conditions. Studies indicate that countries with robust paid leave policies often exhibit lower poverty rates and better health outcomes for children (Puliyel et al., 2021). Such environments foster conditions conducive to educational achievement. For example, Burtle and Bezruchka discuss the implications of parental leave on child health within a broader context of social safety nets, illustrating how a supportive family environment nurtures children's educational engagement (Burtle & Bezruchka, 2016). Additionally, Pratiwi et al. corroborate these findings by arguing that family-friendly human resource management policies, including paid parental leave, significantly contribute to better performance in children (Pratiwi et al., 2023).

In terms of developmental milestones, the availability of paid parental leave allows parents to ensure that their children meet critical early childhood assessments. These assessments are strongly correlated with later academic success. For example, research by Hajizadeh et al. suggests that parental leave facilitates timely childhood vaccinations and health check-ups, which contribute to children's readiness for school (Hajizadeh et al., 2015). This foundational readiness has been linked to improved educational outcomes, demonstrating how health interventions can influence academic metrics later in life (Heymann et al., 2017).

Furthermore, maternal health significantly influences educational outcomes for children. Puliyel et al. emphasize that paid parental leave supports mothers' physical recovery post-birth and reduces incidences of postpartum depression, which can adversely affect maternal engagement with children during formative years (Puliyel et al., 2021). Consequently, the emotional well-being of mothers—supported by paid leave policies—has tremendous implications for children's academic trajectory and social interaction (Nandi et al., 2016).

Beyond maternal and child health improvements, the structural effects of parental leave on family dynamics also warrant attention. Empirical evidence indicates that paid parental leave promotes a more equitable distribution of caregiving responsibilities. This gender equity in parental roles can foster a balanced environment where children receive diverse learning experiences and emotional support from both parents (Lu et al., 2021). This is vital in optimizing children's educational experiences, as diversity in parenting styles is shown to enrich child development and learning (Burtle & Bezruchka, 2016).

It is also critical to consider the implications of these policies within differing socioeconomic contexts. Countries with established paid parental leave comparatively witness heightened adherence to educational benchmarks and improved schooling outcomes, particularly in marginalized communities (Nandi et al., 2016). For example, enrollment rates, performance in standardized tests, and overall academic attainment have been shown to positively correlate with the availability of paid leave, as families can allocate their time and resources more effectively during the crucial early years of a child's education (Bailey et al., 2019).

Moreover, policy advocacy for enhanced parental leave can serve as a catalyst for broader educational initiatives. Advocacy efforts encourage the integration of supportive policies within educational systems, ensuring that children's educational pathways are nurtured from a more stable home environment (Lu et al., 2021). For instance, Bailey et al. found that improved policies could directly expand women's opportunities in the workforce, subsequently benefiting their children's educational prospects (Bailey et al., 2019).

In contrast, the lack of paid parental leave can lead to adverse effects on both child health and academic readiness. The disparities in leave availability often mirror underlying societal inequities, which can hinder children's developmental opportunities (Hawkins, 2020). An analysis by Stack et al. illustrated that residency programs in medicine often lack clear parental leave policies, ultimately disadvantaging trainees and their families during critical child-rearing stages (Stack et al., 2022).

To effectively examine the long-term effects of paid parental leave on children's educational outcomes, further research must consider the multi-dimensional factors influencing both health and education. Longitudinal studies could provide invaluable data on how extended parental leave correlates with educational achievements across diverse populations and various economic contexts.

In summary, the relationship between paid parental leave and children's educational outcomes is deeply interwoven with health, family dynamics, and socioeconomic factors. The advantages that arise from having paid leave are significant, ranging from improved maternal and child health to better academic readiness and long-term educational success. This emphasizes the necessity for policymakers to consider the implementation of comprehensive paid parental leave as a crucial investment in both family health and future educational equity.

Source: Scite for Research (generated 25/04/2025)

# Appendix 5. Commerce Text GenAI Jenni

## Paid parental leave and children's schooling outcomes

The implementation of paid parental leave policies has garnered increasing global attention as a potential mechanism for bolstering early childhood development and fostering greater gender equity in the workforce. These policies, which provide financial support and job protection to parents during the initial period following the birth or adoption of a child, are predicated on the notion that enabling parents to dedicate focused time and attention to their newborns can yield long-term benefits for both the child and the family unit (Wang et al., 2024). Specifically, paid parental leave can facilitate stronger parent-child bonding, promote improved child health outcomes through increased breastfeeding and preventative care, and alleviate financial strain on families during a period of significant adjustment (Heymann et al., 2017). These factors, in turn, are hypothesized to contribute to enhanced cognitive and socio-emotional development in children, setting the stage for improved academic performance and overall well-being as they progress through their schooling years (Stuebe et al., 2024).

The influence of paid parental leave on various aspects of child development and family well-being has been a subject of extensive scholarly investigation, with researchers employing diverse methodological approaches to disentangle the complex relationships at play. Studies have explored the effects of leave duration, benefit levels, and policy design on a range of outcomes, including maternal mental and physical health, breastfeeding rates, child mortality, and early cognitive development (Niel et al., 2020). However, the specific impact of paid parental leave on children's schooling outcomes, such as academic achievement, grade attainment, and educational attainment, remains a relatively underexplored area of research. Understanding the relationship between paid parental leave and schooling outcomes necessitates a nuanced consideration of the multiple pathways through which parental leave policies can exert their influence. One prominent pathway involves the potential for paid parental leave to foster greater parental involvement in their children's education. When parents have access to paid leave, they may be more likely to engage in activities that support their child's learning, such as reading to them, helping with homework, and attending school events.

The impact of paid parental leave on maternal employment patterns is another crucial factor to consider when examining its effects on children's schooling outcomes (Hook & Paek, 2020). Paid leave can facilitate women's return to the workforce after childbirth, which can have positive implications for household income and economic stability (Léopold & Raab, 2010). Furthermore, a mother's continued employment can serve as a positive role model for her children, particularly daughters, potentially influencing their aspirations and educational attainment (Rege & Solli, 2013). However, extended leave durations may also lead to human capital depreciation, impacting productivity and wages (Ruhm, 2011). In addition to these direct effects on parental behavior and family circumstances, paid parental leave policies can also have indirect effects on children's schooling outcomes by influencing the availability and quality of childcare services (Gupta, 2018). In regions with generous paid leave policies, there may be a greater demand for high-quality childcare, leading to investments in early childhood education programs that can benefit children's cognitive and socio-emotional development (Wang et al., 2024).

It is important to acknowledge that the effects of paid parental leave on children's schooling outcomes can vary depending on a multitude of contextual factors, including the socioeconomic status of the family, the cultural norms surrounding parenting, and the specific design features of the leave policy itself. For example, paid parental leave may have a more pronounced impact on children from low-income families, who may be less likely to have access to other resources that support early childhood development. Moreover, the effectiveness of paid parental leave policies in promoting positive schooling outcomes may be contingent on the availability of affordable and high-quality childcare options, as well as supportive workplace policies that enable parents to balance work and family responsibilities. Paid leave policies may increase maternal employment in the short term and potentially continue even after the child is no longer in preschool, as mothers can gain more job skills and strengthen their attachment to the labor force (Cattan, 2016).

The design of parental leave policies themselves, including the length of leave, the level of wage replacement, and the eligibility criteria, can significantly impact their effectiveness. Longer periods of paid leave may allow for more substantial bonding between parents and children, potentially leading to improved developmental outcomes (Casarico & Lattanzio, 2023; Lalive et al., 2013). However, very long leaves may also have unintended consequences, such as hindering women's career progression or creating disincentives for fathers to take leave (Nandi et al., 2018). The level of wage replacement is another critical factor, as it can determine whether low-income families can afford to take advantage of the leave benefit. Furthermore, policies that are inclusive and accessible to all families, regardless of their employment status or family structure, are more likely to have a broad and equitable impact on children's schooling outcomes. The availability of paid sick leave, for instance, has been shown to promote job stability, which is particularly beneficial for families with children (Hill, 2013). Additionally, attitudes toward absenteeism and work ethic should be reevaluated to accommodate worker needs, potentially influencing the utilization of parental leave (Levitt & Barnack-Tavlaris, 2020).

The implementation of paid family leave policies reflects a growing recognition of the importance of work-family balance and the need to support working parents and caregivers (Zambrana et al., 2015). Workplace policies such as paid family leave have been shown to improve employee retention, which can help companies reduce turnover costs (Boushey et al., 2012). Compared to many industrialized nations, the United States lags in providing a balanced lifestyle between work and family life, as it does not offer national paid family leave (Zambrana et al., 2015). Furthermore, family-friendly policies and culture are critical mechanisms for supporting the careers and advancement of women in public service and enhancing gender equity in public sector employment (Feeney & Stritch, 2017). Although the Family and Medical Leave Act of 1993 was a step towards providing national support for families (Pyle & Pelletier, 2004), its limitations in accessibility highlight the need for more comprehensive policies (Scharlach & Grosswald, 1997). Some states have taken the initiative to adopt paid family leave, addressing the gap in national policy and providing valuable support to working families (Wisensale, 2003). Paid leave can yield health and economic benefits for infants, parents, and society, contributing to improved neonatal and maternal outcomes, stronger family relationships, and reduced gender inequalities (Arnautovic & Dammann, 2022; Davison & Blackburn, 2022).

Source: Jenni (generated 25/04/2025)

# Appendix 6. Commerce Text GenAI Yomu

## Paid parental leave and children's schooling outcomes

### Introduction to Paid Parental Leave

Paid parental leave is a policy enabling parents to take a designated period of absence from work following the birth or adoption of a child, during which they receive pay or benefits. This policy aims to support families by allowing parents to bond with their children, adjust to new family dynamics, and facilitate an early healthy development. The growing recognition of the crucial role of early childhood experiences in shaping long-term outcomes has spurred interest in understanding the broader impacts of paid parental leave, including its effects on children's educational attainment.

Governments across the globe have implemented diverse forms of parental leave, with variations in duration, pay rate, and eligibility criteria. These policies are increasingly viewed as significant not only for promoting gender equality in the workplace but also for enhancing children's development outcomes. Researchers aim to unravel how these policies might influence key indicators of child well-being, particularly educational outcomes, given their relevance to personal and societal prosperity.

The investigation of paid parental leave's impact on educational attainment is crucial because it intersects with various policy domains, including education, labor, and family welfare. Understanding this impact requires examining diverse elements such as family socio-economic status, parental involvement in early childhood, and subsequent school environment. Such analysis may guide policymakers in designing effective family support structures.

## Early Developmental Benefits of Paid Parental Leave

The availability of paid parental leave is known to influence children's early development positively. During the crucial first months of life, children undergo rapid neurological development, significantly aided by their interactions with parents. When parents are afforded the time and financial security to spend at home, children benefit from enriched caregiving, fostering cognitive, social, and emotional growth.

Studies suggest that children whose parents could utilize paid parental leave demonstrate advanced developmental milestones compared to those who could not. This progress includes improved language development, better emotional regulation, and higher adaptive behaviors as a result of consistent parental presence. By enabling a nurturing and responsive care environment during infancy, paid leave policies potentially lay a strong foundation for later educational achievements.

Parental leave's impact on early childhood is further enhanced by reducing stressors associated with juggling work and family obligations. Parents who can focus on caregiving without immediate financial strain are better positioned to provide the calm, engaged, and supportive atmosphere ideal for child development. Consequently, reductions in parental stress levels translate to improved parental mental health and, subsequently, more positive parent-child interactions, crucial for setting the stage for successful educational trajectories.

## Long-term Effects on Educational Attainment

As children progress into later stages of learning, the benefits accrued from enhanced early childhood interactions due to paid parental leave continue to manifest. Many studies have established correlations between early childhood stability and later academic success. Access to parental leave policies during early childhood correlates with higher performance in primary and secondary education, as evidenced by improved grades, test scores, and other academic measures.

A critical factor driving these outcomes is the increased capacity of parents to engage in educational activities at home. Parents who have spent more time with their children early in life are more likely to remain involved with their education, supporting learning activities which reinforce school efforts. This continued parental engagement is a key component in sustaining the educational benefits initiated during the period of paid leave.

Moreover, the development of a robust parent-child relationship fostered during the paid leave period enhances children's confidence and motivation. These children tend to exhibit better social skills, higher levels of self-esteem, and a stronger sense of security, all of which are instrumental in navigating the challenges of formal schooling. Thus, paid parental leave's early positive effects extend beyond immediate benefits, fostering long-term improvements in educational attainment and overall well-being.

## Challenges in Measuring the Impact

Despite the potential benefits, measuring the impact of paid parental leave on educational attainment presents several challenges. One significant issue is the diversity in leave policies across different regions which may yield varied outcomes. For instance, countries like Sweden and Norway, with generous leave policies, demonstrate distinctly different educational outcomes compared to countries with limited leave provisions like the United States.

Additionally, variations in socio-economic contexts, cultural norms, and educational systems make it difficult to draw direct comparisons or generalize findings universally. Individual family circumstances, such as parental education levels and poverty status, heavily influence the effectiveness of parental leave benefits. Therefore, while global trends can suggest correlations, local studies are necessary to account for these diverse factors.

Furthermore, parental leave is just one aspect of a multifaceted system influencing educational outcomes. Factors such as quality of early childhood education programs, access to healthcare, and community resources also play pivotal roles. It is essential to consider these factors within the broader context of educational policies to understand the holistic impact of parental leave on children's learning and development. Therefore, policymakers need to integrate insights from varied domains to develop comprehensive strategies that support children's education comprehensively.

## Conclusion: Embracing Comprehensive Parental Leave Policies

In conclusion, the impact of paid parental leave on children's educational attainment underscores the importance of comprehensive family support policies. Early benefits of such policies contribute to richer initial childhood development, setting the stage for later academic success through enhanced parental involvement and secure family environments. These foundational advantages are pivotal in navigating the inevitable challenges of the educational journey.

However, the influence of parental leave cannot be observed in isolation. Successful outcomes depend on a combination of factors, necessitating a coordinated approach to child welfare that encompasses multiple domains. Future research should emphasize longitudinal studies to trace the long-term effects of parental leave policies across diverse socio-economic and cultural contexts.

Adopting well-structured, generous parental leave policies can improve educational outcomes, fostering a more educated, productive, and equitable society. Policymakers are urged to consider these findings when designing family support systems to provide every child with the strongest possible start in life, ultimately benefiting society as a whole.

Source: Yomu (generated 26/04/2025)

# Appendix 7. Law Text GenAI Scite

## Anti-Social Behaviour, Behavioural Expectations and an Urban Aesthetic

The interplay between anti-social behavior, behavioral expectations, and urban aesthetics is critical for understanding how urban environments influence societal interactions. Anti-social behavior encompasses a range of actions that contravene societal norms and expectations, including vandalism, public intoxication, and violence. Meanwhile, behavioral expectations refer to the social norms that dictate acceptable conduct within various contexts.

One fundamental aspect is how urban aesthetics—defined as the visual and sensory qualities of urban spaces—can shape perceptions of safety and community. Research by Millie emphasizes the significance of urban aesthetics in shaping behaviors, noting that aesthetically pleasing environments can deter anti-social activities by fostering a sense of pride and ownership among residents Millie (2007). When urban spaces are well-maintained and visually appealing, they are often associated with enhanced social cohesion, which can reduce the likelihood of anti-social behavior. Conversely, environments marked by neglect and decay can promote feelings of detachment and increase delinquency, as individuals feel less invested in their surroundings.

Aesthetic quality impacts not just individual behaviors but also collective social attitudes. A study highlighted by Kyttä et al. confirms that residents' evaluations of urban aesthetics directly correlate with their perceptions of urban settings' social sustainability (Kyttä et al., 2015). Environments that are visually appealing tend to engender positive emotions and encourage community interactions, further reinforcing behavioral expectations conducive to cohesiveness. For example, when public areas are enhanced with greenery and art, they can serve as gathering spots where prosocial behaviors flourish and negative behaviors diminish.

On the contrary, a lack of aesthetic appeal can lead to diminished social expectations. While the research by Mahat et al. focused on educational environments, it underlines the broader importance of creating engaging environments that can foster positive behaviors and deter potential anti-social actions in urban settings. If residents perceive their public spaces as attractive and well-cared-for, they are more likely to exhibit behaviors aligned with community standards, thus reducing instances of anti-social conduct.

Moreover, behavioral expectations are often informed by the social cues present in urban aesthetics. The design elements of a neighborhood—including lighting, signage, and cleanliness—can signal what behaviors are acceptable. Millie argues that urban designs that prioritize safety and engage community participation can foster an environment where anti-social behavior is less tolerated, resulting in a collective approach to maintaining societal norms. For example, neighborhoods with activated public spaces—such as parks and plazas—encourage community interactions, which can reinforce positive behaviors among residents.

Additionally, social policies and community initiatives play a vital role in shaping these dynamics. The collaborative works of urban planners and local citizens can lead to creating spaces that reflect shared values. Creating aesthetically pleasing environments that also serve functional community purposes (e.g., seating areas, recreational facilities) can fulfill both physical and emotional needs, leading to enhanced community satisfaction and behavioral expectations. Policymakers are encouraged to involve community stakeholders in urban design processes, ensuring that aesthetic improvements align with public expectations and contribute to social cohesion.

Community spaces that invite participation and interaction are pivotal for creating environments where anti-social behavior is less likely to occur. Environments devoid of public engagement opportunities tend to foster isolation, where anti-social behavior may thrive due to lack of accountability and social monitoring. Research indicates that perceived social support networks can shape individual behaviors, thus highlighting the need to design urban environments that promote consistent social engagement.

Addressing behavioral expectations through urban aesthetics also necessitates a lens on diversity and inclusion. Aesthetic strategies that encompass diverse cultural expressions can ensure broad community engagement and participation, enabling a sense of belonging among varying demographic groups. Inclusive urban design can diminish feelings of disenfranchisement that often lead to anti-social behaviors, as residents feel represented and valued within their shared environment.

Moreover, the impact of urban aesthetics on anti-social behavior reflects broader societal issues. Aesthetic neglect in urban areas often mirrors systemic inequities, where marginalized communities are disproportionately affected by deteriorating surroundings that can amplify anti-social tendencies. Addressing these inequities through targeted aesthetic interventions and community investment becomes imperative in reshaping behavioral expectations and fostering healthier social interactions.

The link between urban aesthetics and anti-social behavior extends to crime prevention strategies as well. Research highlights how well-lit and maintained urban spaces tend to correlate with lower crime rates. Environments that prioritize safety features through aesthetics, such as increased visibility and accessibility, can reduce opportunities for anti-social behavior. Creating spaces that feel secure and inviting can deter those who might otherwise engage in delinquent acts.

Furthermore, the role of social norms is underscored within this discussion. When communal investment in maintaining aesthetic standards exists, behavioral expectations are subsequently reinforced. Residents in visually pleasing environments may establish informal social rules that discourage anti-social conduct, thereby instilling a community-driven approach to preventing negative behaviors. Initiatives that involve community members in aesthetic maintenance—such as neighborhood clean-ups or beautification projects—can further foster a shared commitment to upholding positive behavior expectations.

Involving community members in urban design and maintenance processes can catalyze engagement and ownership. Millie posits that resident participation in aesthetic discussions enhances the likelihood of adherence to cooperative behavioral norms, creating an environment where anti-social behaviors are actively combated. This proactive involvement reinforces the value of collective responsibility and empowers communities to take action against behaviors that threaten social cohesion.

The public perception of urban space aesthetics can significantly influence behavioral expectations. Place-making initiatives can enhance the social value of urban spaces by encouraging positive community interactions. When urban aesthetics foster positive experiences, they can contribute to a culture of mutual respect and engagement that diminishes the acceptance of anti-social behavior (Alzahrani et al., 2017).

In summary, the relationship between anti-social behavior, behavioral expectations, and urban aesthetics is intricately woven into the fabric of communal life. Urban environments that prioritize aesthetics not only enhance visual appeal but also foster safe, engaging spaces that promote positive behaviors and reduce anti-social conduct. Investing in aesthetic qualities and understanding the social dynamics within urban settings are crucial for promoting healthier community interactions and nurturing a sense of shared responsibility. As urban planners and policymakers integrate aesthetic considerations with community needs, the potential for fostering environments that combat anti-social tendencies becomes increasingly feasible.

Source: Scite for Research (generated 25/04/2025)

# Appendix 8. Law Text GenAI Jenni

## Anti-Social Behaviour, Behavioural Expectations and an Urban Aesthetic

Urban spaces are increasingly being shaped by aesthetic considerations, with new developments often harnessing aesthetic experiences to reinforce social hierarchies and exclusion (Rothenberg & Lang, 2015). The pursuit of aesthetic experiences has become a common phenomenon, warranting a reevaluation of its exclusive association with privileged urban groups and its potential to overlook the experiences of marginalized communities (Guano, 2020). Aesthetics are multifaceted, encompassing Populuxe, Minimalistic, Modernist, Postmodern, Social, Environmental, Sustainable, Economic, Feminist, Native American, African, and Asian forms, highlighting its cultural relativity in our globalized world (Ghom & George, 2021). Moreover, the performance of built forms is intrinsically linked to aesthetics, subject to objective assessment through cost-benefit analyses, especially in light of mandatory performance requirements like energy efficiency, carbon footprint reduction, sustainability, and indoor air quality (Langhorst, 2014). This intricate interplay between aesthetics and performance is evident in the de-aestheticization of contemporary conceptual art, where the emphasis shifts from physical objects in museums to ongoing events and situations that defy commodification, embodying a resistance to the commodification of art and prompting a reevaluation of artistic value in contemporary society (Kui-ying, 2022). The urban aesthetic can be further understood through the lens of postmodernism, which has inspired practitioners to explore the functions and aesthetics of public spaces (Nagaynay & Lee, 2020). Such exploration encompasses elements like roads, squares, parks, and service areas, as well as tangible and intangible aspects of urban design, including environmental consciousness, technological integration, and the cultivation of cultural identities (Gao & Song-fu, 2021).

Aesthetic considerations in urban design carry significant implications for social behavior and expectations, particularly in relation to anti-social behavior. Vandalism, for instance, is a significant issue in urban environments and is strongly influenced by the physical quality of the environment and locational factors (Yavuz & n, 2011). Street art, a form of creative expression commonly found in public spaces, contributes to the physical sustainability of the built environment by enhancing the livability of buildings and urban infrastructures for all city dwellers (Forte & Paola, 2019). Urban planning has shifted from space theory to ecological theory, emphasizing "Design with Nature" from an ecological and holistic perspective, thus aesthetic visual ecology can humanize and reshape the urban landscape (Chu, 2011). Architects play a crucial role in designing comfortable, harmonious environments that incorporate new requirements and technologies, shaping the urban environment through building design, landscaping, color and lighting solutions, advertising, and decorative elements (Месенева, 2020). The urban landscape serves as a physical space for the operation of materials and the formation of comprehensive artistic expression, highlighting the intrinsic connection between urban landscape design and various art forms (Yong, 2014). Urban design profoundly influences the quality of life for city dwellers, including their mental health, by shaping the spaces in which people live, work, and interact, and can foster a sense of community and belonging (Olszewska-Guizzo et al., 2021).

The concept of urban sustainability is defined as a multi-layered concept where aesthetics are as important as economic viability or ecological value (Roggema, 2016). By integrating architecture and planning, urban design structures buildings to form a single composition to improve social, cultural, economic, and environmental aspects (Sushanti et al., 2020; Zavrl & Zeren, 2010). The design of sustainable buildings encompasses social sustainability, concentrating on the relationship between buildings and their occupants, with considerations for health, comfort, flexibility, adaptability, and accessibility. This approach aligns with the principles of green development, which aims to transform cities from consumers to energy producers by utilizing their resources and emphasizing green infrastructure for biomass production (Khaleefah & Alwan, 2022). Furthermore, the aestheticization of the environment plays a crucial role in both nature conservation and urban planning by offering a philosophical means of integrating culture, history, and environmental ethics, potentially turning environmental protection into an aesthetic project. Garden landscape design is closely intertwined with aesthetics, environmental science, and planning technology, and it encompasses various aspects such as scenic spot planning, road environment design, community greening, and urban greening (Sun & Yang, 2021).

The dynamic relationship between urban aesthetics and human behavior is further mediated by cultural and social factors, with cultural landscapes emerging from the interaction between human activities and the natural environment (Permyakov & Krasnova, 2019). Landscape architecture research increasingly emphasizes the interaction between restorative landscapes, physical space environments, and behavioral space environments, highlighting the critical role of landscape design in promoting public health (Liu et al., 2023). To improve the urban environment and promote harmony between humans and nature, the concept of ecological aesthetics is introduced to guide urban landscape architecture practices (Ņitavska et al., 2020). The harmonious integration of architecture with its surrounding landscape is a key principle of sustainable design, underscoring the importance of aesthetics in creating environmentally responsible and socially equitable urban spaces (He & Nie, 2014). When designing new buildings and planning future cities, architects should address the human desire for harmonious interaction with nature while also showcasing the historical characteristics of buildings, which are connected to fundamental human feelings and emotions and can improve the holistic relationships between buildings and nature. This can be achieved through nature-inspired designs that incorporate elements like trees, flowers, and natural patterns to evoke emotional responses and enhance the overall aesthetic experience (Kim & Park, 2018).

The perception of aesthetics within urban environments is shaped by individual experiences, cultural backgrounds, and social contexts, ultimately influencing behavior and expectations in a variety of ways. Urban spaces are not merely physical entities but are also social constructs that reflect and reinforce societal values and norms (Qiu & Pan, 2023). The attractiveness of urban environments has been linked to restorative components, with open and luminous spaces conducive to leisure and social interactions being particularly favored (Pazhouhanfar & Kamal, 2013). This underscores the importance of incorporating nature and green spaces into urban design, as they offer opportunities for relaxation, recreation, and social engagement, ultimately contributing to the well-being of city residents (Andreucci et al., 2019). Integrating green spaces into urban design is crucial for promoting environmental, aesthetic, recreational, and economic benefits, but these spaces are diminishing due to urban growth (Nshimiyimana et al., 2023). It is important to consider the qualitative perspective of sound which includes sonic diversity and acoustic ecology, which is a neglected area of urban design (Rehan, 2015).

The principles of ecological dynamics provide a framework for understanding how urban nature environments can be designed to promote health and well-being, highlighting the importance of considering both natural and built features. Biophilic design principles can be applied to create urban spaces that connect people with nature, which involves direct experiences of nature, such as natural light and vegetation, and indirect experiences, such as views of nature (Tabassum & Park, 2024). These biophilic elements can be incorporated into the renewal of conventional streets and the design of new ones, creating multiple urban benefits. In these spaces, the bond between people and nature is nurtured, increasing the likelihood that residents will protect and save urban green spaces (Cabanek et al., 2020). Urban design should consider the psychological needs of city dwellers, such as the need for pleasant areas, security, and social interaction, to ensure that urban spaces are both sustainable and supportive of human well-being (Gifford & Sussman, 2012).

Source: Jenni (generated 25/04/2025)

# Appendix 9. Law Text GenAI Yomu

## Anti-Social Behaviour, Behavioural Expectations and an Urban Aesthetic

### Introduction to Anti-Social Behavior and Urban Aesthetics

Anti-social behavior in urban environments is a complex issue that encompasses a range of activities deemed socially disruptive and harmful to community well-being. These behaviors can include vandalism, public intoxication, and noise disturbances, which directly affect the urban aesthetic by degrading the physical and social environment. The interplay between these behaviors and urban aesthetics is significant and complex, as cities strive to balance the enforcement of behavioral norms with the creation of inclusive and vibrant public spaces.

Urban aesthetics refer to the visual and sensory landscape of urban areas, which is shaped by architecture, public art, green spaces, and cleanliness. These components contribute to the overall quality of life and community perception of safety and orderliness. Anti-social behavior often poses a threat to this aesthetic by introducing elements of neglect and disorder. Thus, understanding the interaction between anti-social behavior and urban aesthetics is crucial for urban planners and policymakers.

Moreover, the expectations for urban aesthetics vary across different communities and cultural contexts. These expectations can influence what is considered anti-social behavior, as certain activities may be more acceptable in one cultural setting than in another. Consequently, defining what constitutes anti-social behavior often depends on the prevailing cultural and contextual norms of specific urban areas. This dynamic highlights the necessity of considering local cultural values when addressing anti-social behavior in urban spaces.

## The Impact of Anti-Social Behavior on Urban Areas

Anti-social behavior can significantly disrupt the visual and psychological appeal of urban spaces. Vandalism, such as graffiti on historical monuments or modern structures, detracts from the visual harmony and intended purpose of urban design. This type of behavior not only diminishes the aesthetic appeal but also incurs financial costs associated with cleaning and restoration. The prevalence of vandalism can lead to a heightened perception of disorder, which may discourage community engagement and tourism.

Public intoxication and noise disturbances are other forms of anti-social behavior that negatively impact urban environments. These behaviors can make public spaces feel unsafe and unwelcoming, reducing their usability and leading to social isolation among residents. Spaces like parks and public squares are designed to foster social interaction and community cohesion; when these spaces are dominated by disruptive behaviors, their intended purpose is compromised.

Moreover, the persistence of anti-social behavior in urban settings can perpetuate a cycle of neglect and decay. Areas frequently subjected to such behavior may experience a decline in property values and a reduction in business investment. This decline can result in diminished resources for local governments to maintain and improve public spaces, further eroding the urban aesthetic and reinforcing the cycle of neglect. Addressing the root causes of anti-social behavior, therefore, is vital to preserving urban aesthetics and promoting sustainable urban development.

## The Role of Behavioral Norms in Shaping Urban Spaces

Behavioral norms play a critical role in shaping the character and use of urban spaces. These norms are often unwritten but widely understood rules that govern acceptable behavior in public environments. Communities develop these norms based on shared values and cultural practices, which help maintain order and predictability in urban settings. When individuals adhere to these norms, urban spaces can function effectively and equitably, facilitating conducive environments for social interaction and economic activities.

The enforcement of behavioral norms is vital in preventing anti-social behavior and maintaining urban aesthetics. Law enforcement agencies, community organizations, and local governments are key players in this process, employing strategies such as surveillance, community policing, and educational campaigns to encourage compliance. By promoting restorative justice and community engagement, cities can reduce incidences of anti-social behavior, thus preserving the urban aesthetic and enhancing the overall quality of life.

However, the imposition of strict behavioral norms can also lead to exclusion and gentrification. When too rigidly enforced, these norms may marginalize certain groups, whose cultural expressions and behaviors might not align with mainstream expectations. It is important for policymakers to strike a balance between upholding behavioral norms that contribute to safety and aesthetics, and allowing for diversity and inclusivity in urban spaces. This balance can transform urban environments into more dynamic and resilient communities.

### Conclusion: Balancing Aesthetics and Inclusivity in Urban Management

In conclusion, the relationship between anti-social behavior and urban aesthetics is multifaceted and deeply interconnected with behavioral norms. Anti-social behaviors pose a significant challenge to urban aesthetics by affecting both the visual and functional quality of urban spaces. These challenges necessitate proactive strategies from urban planners and community leaders to enforce behavioral norms that preserve the urban aesthetic, while also fostering inclusivity.

Understanding and respecting community-specific behavioral norms can enhance urban management efforts. By aligning urban policies with local cultural values and norms, cities can effectively mitigate the impact of anti-social behavior and improve the urban aesthetic. This approach helps ensure that urban spaces remain vibrant, welcoming, and inclusive for a diverse population.

Ultimately, the successful management of urban spaces requires a nuanced understanding of the complex interplay between anti-social behavior, behavioral norms, and urban aesthetics. By prioritizing both aesthetics and inclusivity, urban planners can create sustainable environments that encourage positive social interactions and contribute to the well-being of urban communities.

Source: Yomu (generated 26/04/2025)

# Appendix 10. Science Text GenAI Scite

## Risk of yellow fever virus transmission in the Asia-Pacific region

The risk of yellow fever virus (YFV) transmission in the Asia-Pacific region is a growing concern, particularly due to ongoing globalization, international travel, and increasing vector activity. Despite the historical absence of yellow fever in this region, several environmental and ecological factors indicate a potential vulnerability to YFV outbreaks.

The Aedes aegypti mosquito, which is an efficient vector for YFV, has established itself in many tropical and subtropical regions, including parts of Asia. The presence of Aedes spp. does not directly correlate with the transmission of yellow fever; however, the density of these mosquito populations in urban areas poses a concerning risk factor. Urbanization often leads to increased human-mosquito interaction, creating opportunities for viral transmission if the virus were introduced through travel (Shearer et al., 2018; Shinde et al., 2024). Countries like China, which have documented imported cases of YFV, demonstrate the potential for local transmission if epidemiological conditions align (Kuno, 2020; Zhao et al., 2018).

Modeling analyses suggest that cities in Asia with high populations and established Aedes mosquito populations are particularly vulnerable to YFV introduction, especially following the patterns of past dengue virus transmission (Brent et al., 2018; Lataillade et al., 2020). The ecological models used in these studies identify areas typically infected by dengue virus as simultaneously at risk for yellow fever due to the similar transmission pathways shared by both viruses (Brent et al., 2018). Moreover, increased international travel patterns raise the risk of YFV importation from endemic regions, especially when travelers transmit the virus to densely populated areas that have not previously encountered it (Tomori, 2004; Johansson et al., 2012).

There are intricate dynamics surrounding population immunity and vector control that further complicate yellow fever transmission in the Asia-Pacific region. Countries like Sri Lanka have issued health alerts for potential yellow fever outbreaks, indicating a vulnerability compounded by low vaccination rates and high mosquito densities (Agampodi & Wickramage, 2013). Immunologically naive populations, coupled with favorable ecological conditions for mosquito vectors, could theoretically catalyze urban outbreaks if the virus were to establish itself locally (Chippaux & Chippaux, 2018).

The efficacy of yellow fever vaccination programs has historically controlled prevalence in endemic regions; however, their application and coverage vary significantly in the Asia-Pacific region. Recent reviews highlight a substantial gap in vaccination among populations in proximity to known vectors in Asia, potentially exacerbating risks during outbreaks (Shearer et al., 2017; Barnett et al., 2008). The disparities in vaccination coverage create populations that lack immunity; in light of climate change, which affects vector habitat suitability, the risk of yellow fever emergence could substantially increase (Fraser et al., 2024; Aliaga-Samanez et al., 2023).

The absence of historical yellow fever epidemics in Asia may stem from specific ecological and viral factors that have not yet been elucidated. For instance, while Aedes aegypti mosquitoes thrive in Asia, yellow fever has not been able to establish itself. This raises questions about ecological constraints on viral transmission or potential cross-immunity from other flaviviruses circulating in the region, like dengue and Zika, which may inhibit yellow fever virus replication (Clements & Harbach, 2017; Shinde et al., 2024).

Importantly, the role of sylvatic cycles of transmission, which occur in forest-dwelling non-human primates, has been indicated as a vector in sustaining yellow fever in endemic regions. These cycles are less understood in Asia and could be crucial in understanding potential emergence (Valentine et al., 2019). There remains a need for extensive surveillance of non-human primate populations and mosquito vectors in Asia to ascertain the risk of domestic transmission should the virus find its way into human populations.

Monitoring efforts should also consider climate change projections that predict shifts in vector distribution, thereby increasing the likelihood of yellow fever's introduction. Models forecasting ecological niches suggest that areas conducive to Aedes mosquito proliferation could expand, presenting heightened risks of transmission (Fraser et al., 2024; Aliaga-Samanez et al., 2023). The intertwining relationships between climate variables, urbanization, and human mobility heighten the urgency for multifaceted strategies to mitigate potential outbreaks.

In conclusion, the Asia-Pacific region exhibits a complex web of risk concerning yellow fever virus transmission. Factors such as increasing urbanization, intense human-mosquito interactions, varying vaccination rates, and ecological biodiversity provide a fertile ground for potential outbreaks. Integrated surveillance programs and vaccination strategies, along with understanding the interplay of climate change and vector ecology, are paramount for preemptively managing the risks of yellow fever in this region.

Source: Scite for Research (generated 25/04/2025)

# Appendix 11. Science Text GenAI: Jenni

## Risk of yellow fever virus transmission in the Asia-Pacific region

The Asia-Pacific region, encompassing a vast archipelago of diverse ecosystems and densely populated urban centers, faces a significant yet often overlooked threat from yellow fever virus. While yellow fever is not currently endemic in the region, the potential for its introduction and subsequent transmission is a growing concern due to several converging factors (Ortiz-Martínez et al., 2017). Increased global travel and trade, coupled with the presence of competent mosquito vectors such as Aedes aegypti and Aedes albopictus, create pathways for the virus to enter and establish itself in new areas (Ramachari & Purushothaman, 2019). The ecological and epidemiological landscape of the Asia-Pacific region shares similarities with areas in Africa and the Americas where yellow fever is endemic, heightening the risk of its emergence (Espinal et al., 2019). Understanding the interplay of vector biology, environmental drivers, and human behavior is crucial for assessing the risk of yellow fever virus transmission in the Asia-Pacific region and implementing effective preventive measures (Abdullahi et al., 2021). The absence of widespread immunity to yellow fever in the human population of the Asia-Pacific region further exacerbates the potential for large-scale outbreaks if the virus is introduced (Irsal et al., 2023; Nakase et al., 2024).

The changing global climate plays a crucial role in shaping the geographical distribution and activity of mosquito vectors, with rising temperatures and altered rainfall patterns potentially expanding their range and breeding seasons (Davis et al., 2021). Such shifts in vector ecology could create new areas of vulnerability within the Asia-Pacific region, increasing the likelihood of yellow fever virus transmission should the virus be introduced (Ramadhani & Latif, 2021). Moreover, the rapid urbanization and associated environmental changes in many parts of the Asia-Pacific region can create ideal breeding grounds for Aedes mosquitoes, further amplifying the risk. Dengue epidemics have occurred in various regions of the world, and with no treatment or vaccine, controlling the vector by destroying habitats becomes crucial (Madeira et al., 2002). The increasing interconnectedness of the world through travel and commerce facilitates the movement of both infected humans and vectors, potentially introducing the virus into previously unaffected areas (Carrington & Simmons, 2014; Wilder-Smith et al., 2013). Surveillance systems need to be strengthened to detect and respond to any incursion of yellow fever virus promptly. Public health infrastructure and response capacity are critical for managing potential outbreaks and mitigating their impact.

The introduction of the yellow fever virus into the Asia-Pacific region could have devastating consequences, given the high population density and the potential for rapid spread in the absence of widespread immunity. Factors such as vector efficiency, viral infectivity, and environmental variables play a role in the transmission of dengue in different regions (Were, 2012). Furthermore, socioeconomic factors such as poverty, inadequate sanitation, and limited access to healthcare can exacerbate the impact of outbreaks, particularly in vulnerable populations. Therefore, proactive measures such as strengthening vector control programs, enhancing surveillance systems, and promoting vaccination in high-risk areas are essential to prevent the establishment and spread of yellow fever in the Asia-Pacific region. Understanding the mosquito's spread in the environment is important for implementing effective control strategies (Fonzi et al., 2015). These measures should be tailored to the specific ecological and epidemiological characteristics of different sub-regions within the Asia-Pacific region, considering factors such as vector species distribution, climate patterns, and population density.

Effective vector control strategies, including the use of insecticides, larval source reduction, and community-based mosquito control programs, are essential for reducing the risk of yellow fever virus transmission. Integrated vector management approaches, which combine multiple control methods in a coordinated and sustainable manner, are particularly effective in reducing vector populations and minimizing the risk of arbovirus transmission. Further research is needed to evaluate the effectiveness of different vector control strategies in the specific context of the Asia-Pacific region, taking into account the local vector species, environmental conditions, and community practices. Chemical, environmental, and biological methods are some of the ways to control vector populations (Ogunlade et al., 2021).

The development and deployment of effective yellow fever vaccines are critical for preventing outbreaks and protecting populations at risk. Vaccination campaigns should be targeted at high-risk populations, such as travelers to endemic areas and residents of areas with suitable vector populations and environmental conditions. Furthermore, the development of new and improved yellow fever vaccines, including those that are safer, more effective, and easier to administer, is an important priority for global health research. It is essential to invest in research to better understand the factors that drive yellow fever virus transmission in the Asia-Pacific region and to develop evidence-based strategies for prevention and control. This includes research on vector ecology, virus evolution, human behavior, and the impact of climate change on disease transmission dynamics.

Source: Jenni AI (generated 25/04/2025)

# Appendix 12. Science Text GenAI Yomu

## Risk of yellow fever virus transmission in the Asia-Pacific region

### Introduction to Yellow Fever Virus

Yellow fever is a viral infection transmitted by mosquitoes, primarily affecting humans and nonhuman primates. It is endemic to parts of Africa and South America and is caused by a virus belonging to the Flavivirus genus. This disease is characterized by a sudden onset of fever, chills, muscle pain, headache, nausea, and fatigue. In severe cases, it can lead to jaundice, bleeding, and potentially fatal kidney and liver impairment.

Historically, the Asia-Pacific region, encompassing countries such as China, India, Japan, Indonesia, and others, remains free of yellow fever despite the prevalence of suitable environmental conditions and vectors like Aedes mosquitoes, which theoretically could support the virus. The absence of the virus in this heavily populated area raises questions regarding future risks, especially in the context of increased global travel and changing climate patterns.

Given the region's exposure to other mosquito-borne diseases like dengue and Zika, assessing the risk of yellow fever virus transmission in the Asia-Pacific region becomes increasingly relevant. This assessment involves understanding the prerequisites for transmission, the potential impact of environmental and anthropogenic factors, and strategic control measures to prevent an outbreak from occurring.

### Transmission Prerequisites

For the yellow fever virus to establish transmission in a new region, certain conditions must be met. Firstly, the region should have competent mosquito vectors, such as Aedes aegypti or Aedes albopictus, that can sustain yellow fever virus transmission. These mosquito species are prevalent throughout the Asia-Pacific, contributing to the transmission of other arboviruses, indicating the risk if yellow fever were introduced.

Human movement, including travel and trade, is another key factor. International travel can facilitate the introduction of the virus by an infected individual who travels to the Asia-Pacific region. Given the ease of travel and the volume of people moving in and out of the region, the possibility of introducing the virus is a significant concern. Airports hosting international flights are settings with elevated risk for the entry of yellow fever due to arriving travelers.

To establish transmission chains, the virus must also circulate within a community. Therefore, continuous transmission would require an area with sufficient human hosts, conducive urban or peri-urban environments, and a humid climate to foster large mosquito populations. The densely populated and rapidly urbanizing cities of the Asia-Pacific fulfill these conditions, making them potential hotspots if yellow fever were to be introduced.

## Environmental and Anthropogenic Influences

The warm and humid climates of the Asia-Pacific region provide an ideal environment for mosquito breeding and survival, facilitating the transmission of vector-borne diseases. The presence of widespread vector habitats, ranging from urban landscapes with artificial water containers to rural areas with natural breeding sites, enhances the potential for yellow fever virus transmission.

Climate change poses an additional risk by altering the ecological equilibrium, possibly increasing both the geographic range and the seasonality of mosquito populations. As global temperatures rise, regions that were once too cool for Aedes mosquitoes may become conducive to their survival and proliferation. Consequently, areas within the Asia-Pacific region might see a rise in mosquito populations, elevating the risk of dengue and potentially yellow fever outbreaks.

Anthropogenic activities, such as deforestation and urban sprawl, disrupt natural habitats and bring human settlements closer to primate populations, which are natural yellow fever reservoirs. This habitat disturbance increases human exposure to potential wildlife transmission cycles. Furthermore, these activities often result in poor sanitation and water storage practices, providing numerous mosquito breeding grounds, thereby increasing transmission risk.

## Potential Control Measures

One of the most effective control measures to prevent the introduction and spread of yellow fever is vaccination. The World Health Organization recommends the vaccination of travelers moving from yellow fever endemic regions to non-endemic areas, such as the Asia-Pacific, to prevent the virus's entry. Additionally, ensuring high vaccination coverage in endemic regions reduces the number of potential carriers who might travel.

Vector control strategies remain crucial in regions at risk of arbovirus introductions. Effective practices include environmental management to eliminate mosquito breeding sites, the use of insecticides, and community participation to promote public health awareness regarding mosquito control and personal protection. These strategies help reduce the mosquito population and interrupt potential transmission chains.

Combating the risk of yellow fever in the Asia-Pacific also requires robust surveillance and early warning systems. Monitoring disease patterns and vector density can provide timely alerts that facilitate rapid response measures. Cross-border collaborations, sharing epidemiological data, and conducting joint research initiatives with yellow fever endemic countries can strengthen preparedness and response capabilities.

## Conclusion

The risk of yellow fever virus emerging in the Asia-Pacific region cannot be overlooked given the presence of competent vectors, a suitable environment, and the potential for human-mediated virus introduction. The assessment highlights the necessity for vigilance in monitoring factors that contribute to virus transmission and implementing strategic preventative measures, such as vaccination, vector control, and surveillance.

Environmental changes and human activities that favor the proliferation of mosquito vectors necessitate a proactive approach to epidemic preparedness. By understanding the dynamics of risk and the methods of mitigation, public health authorities can fortify the region's defenses against potential outbreaks.

In conclusion, assessing and managing the risk of yellow fever transmission requires an integrated approach that combines environmental, public health, and policy perspectives to safeguard the Asia-Pacific region from this potentially deadly virus.

Source: Yomu (generated 26/04/2025)

# Appendix 13. Headwords of the GSL KI List

This list contains the headwords of the word families appearing in the K1 word list based on West's (1953) GSL (Nation, 2025)

a
able
about
above
accept
accord
account
across
act
actual
add
address
admit
adopt
advance
advantage
affair
afford
after
again
against
age
ago
agree
air
all
allow
almost
alone
along
already
also
although
always
among
amount
ancient
and
animal
another
answer
any
appear
apply
appoint
arise
arm
army
around
arrive
art
article
as
ask
association
at
attack
attempt
average
away
back
bad
ball
bank
bar
base
battle
be
bear

beauty
because
become
bed
before
begin
behind
being
believe
belong
below
beneath
beside
best
better
between
beyond
big
bill
bird
bit
black
blood
blow
blue
board
boat
body
book
born
both
box
boy
branch
bread
breadth
break
bridge
bright
bring
brother
build
burn
business
but
buy
by
call
can
capital
car
care
carry
case
catch
cause
centre
certain
chance
change
character
charge
chief
child
choose
church
circle
city
claim
class
clean
clear
clock
close
club
coast
cold
college
colour
come
command
common
company
compare
complete
concern
condition
connect
consider
contain
content
continue
control
corner
cost
could
council
count
country
course
court
cover
creature
cross
crowd
cry
current
custom
cut
dance
danger
dare
dark
date
daughter
day
dead

deal
decide
declare
deep
degree
deliver
demand
describe
desert
desire
destroy
detail
determine
develop
die
difference
difficult
direct
discover
disease
distance
distinguish
district
divide
do
doctor
dog
door
double
doubt
down
draw
dream
dress
drive
drop
dry
due
during
each
ear
early
earth
east
easy
eat
edge
effect
effort
either
else
employ
end
enemy
English
enjoy
enough
enter
entire
equal
escape
even
evening
event
ever
every
everywhere
evil
example
excellent
except
exchange
exercise
exist
expect
expense
experience
experiment
explain
express
extend
eye
face
fact
factory
fail
fair
faith
fall
familiar
family
famous
farm
fashion
fast
father
favourite
favour
fear
feed
feel
fellow
few
field
figure
fill
find
fine
finger
finish
fire
first
fish
fit
fix
floor
flower

follow
food
for
force
foreign
forget
form
former
forth
fortune
forward
free
friend
from
front
full
further
future
gain
game
garden
gate
gather
general
gentle
get
give
glad
glass
go
gold
good
great
green
ground
group
grow
guard
habit
half
hall
hand
handle
hang
happen
happy
hard
hardly
have
he
head
health
hear
heat
heaven
heavy
help
her
here
hide
high
hill
his
history
hold
home
honour
hope
horse
hot
hour
house
how
hullo
human
hurrah
husband
I
idea
if
impossible
in
inch
include
increase
indeed
independent
influence
instead
intend
interest
into
introduce
iron
it
its
join
judge
just
keep
kill
kind
know
lack
lady
land
language
large
last
late
law
lay
lead
learn
least
leave
left

length
less
let
letter
level
library
lie
life
lift
light
like
likely
limit
line
listen
little
live
local
long
look
lose
lost
lot
love
low
machine
main
make
man
manner
manners
many
march
mark
market
marry
mass
material
matter
may
me
mean
measure
meet
member
memory
mention
mere
metal
middle
might
mile
mind
mine
minister
minute
miss
modern
moment
money
month
more
moreover
morning
most
mother
motor
mountain
mouth
move
much
music
must
my
name
narrow
nation
native
nature
near
necessary
neck
need
neighbour
neither
never
new
next
night
no
none
nor
north
not
note
nothing
notice
now
nowhere
number
object
observe
occasion
of
off
offer
office
often
oil
old
once
one
only
open
operation
opinion
opportunity

or
order
ordinary
organize
other
otherwise
ought
ounce
our
out
over
owe
own
page
pain
paint
paper
part
party
pass
past
pay
peace
people
perfect
perhaps
permanent
permit
person
picture
piece
place
plan
plant
play
please
point
political
poor
popular
population
position
possess
possible
post
pound
poverty
power
practical
prepare
present
preserve
press
pretty
prevent
price
print
private
problem
produce
product
production
program
programme
progress
promise
proof
proper
propose
protect
prove
provide
public
pull
purpose
put
quality
quarter
quiet
quite
race
raise
rank
rate
rather
reach
read
ready
real
reason
receive
recent
recognize
record
red
reduce
refuse
regard
regular
relation
religion
remain
remark
remember
repeat
reply
report
represent
respect
rest
result
return
rich
ride
right
ring
rise

river
road
roll
room
rough
round
rule
ruler
run
rush
safe
sail
same
save
saw
say
scale
scarce
scene
school
science
sea
season
seat
second
secret
secretary
see
seem
seize
sell
send
sense
separate
serious
serve
set
settle
several
shadow
shake
shall
shape
share
shave
she
shine
shoe
shoot
shore
short
should
shoulder
show
side
sight
sign
silence
silver
simple
since
single
sir
sister
sit
situation
size
skill
sky
sleep
slight
slow
small
smile
so
society
soft
soil
some
son
soon
sort
sound
south
space
speak
special
speed
spend
spirit
spite
spot
spread
spring
square
stage
stand
standard
start
state
station
stay
steal
steel
step
stick
still
stock
stone
stop
store
storm
story
straight
strange
stream
street

strength
stretch
strike
strong
struggle
study
subject
substance
succeed
such
sudden
suffer
suggest
summer
sun
supply
support
suppose
sure
surface
surprise
surround
sweet
system
table
take
talk
taste
teach
tear
tell
term
terrible
test
than
that
the
their
them
then
there
therefore
these
they
thing
think
this
though
thought
through
throw
thus
time
to
today
together
too
top
total
touch
toward
town
trade
train
travel
tree
trouble
trust
truth
try
turn
type
under
understand
union
unite
university
unless
until
up
upon
use
usual
valley
value
various
very
view
village
visit
voice
vote
wait
walk
wall
want
war
warn
waste
watch
water
wave
way
we
weak
wear
week
welcome
well
west
what
when
where
whether
which
while
white

who
whose
why
wide
wife
wild
will
win
wind
window
wing
winter
wise
wish
with
within
without
woman
wonder
wood
word
work
world
worse
worth
would
write
wrong
year
yellow
yes
yesterday
yet
you
young

# Appendix 14. Headwords of the GSL K2 List

This list contains the headwords of the word families appearing in the K2 word list based on West's (1953) GSL (Nation, 2025).

abroad
absence
absolutely
accident
accuse
accustom
ache
admire
adventure
advertise
advice
afraid
afternoon
agent
agriculture
ahead
aim
aeroplane
alike
alive
aloud
altogether
ambition
amongst
amuse
anger
angle
annoy
anxiety
apart
apologize
applaud
apple
approve
arch
argue
arrange
arrest
arrow
artificial
ash
ashamed
aside
asleep
astonish
attend
attract
audience
aunt
autumn
avenue
avoid
awake
awkward
axe
baby
bag
baggage
bake
balance
band
barber
bare
bargain
barrel
basin
basket
bath
bay

beak
beam
bean
beard
beast
beat
beg
behave
bell
belt
bend
berry
bicycle
bind
birth
bite
bitter
blade
blame
bless
blind
block
boast
boil
bold
bone
border
borrow
bottle
bottom
bound
boundary
bow
bowl
brain
brass
brave
breakfast
breath
bribe
brick
broad
brown
brush
bucket
bunch
bundle
burst
bury
bus
bush
busy
butter
button
cage
cake
calculate
calm
camera
camp
canal
cap
cape
captain
card
carriage
cart
castle
cat
cattle
caution
cave
cent
century
ceremony
chain
chair
chalk
charm
cheap
cheat
check
cheer
cheese
cheque
chest
chicken
chimney
Christmas
civilize
clay
clerk
clever
cliff
climb
cloth
cloud
coal
coarse
coat
coffee
coin
collar
collect
colony
comb
combine
comfort
commerce
committee
companion
compete
complain
complicated
compose
confess
confidence

confuse
congratulate
conquer
conscience
conscious
convenience
conversation
cook
cool
copper
copy
cork
corn
correct
cottage
cotton
cough
courage
cousin
cow
coward
crack
crash
cream
creep
crime
critic
crop
crown
cruel
crush
cultivate
cup
cupboard
cure
curious
curl
curse
curtain
curve
cushion
damage
damp
deaf
dear
debt
decay
deceive
decrease
deed
deer
defeat
defend
delay
delicate
delight
department
depend
descend
deserve
desk
despair
devil
diamond
dictionary
dig
dinner
dip
dirt
disappoint
discipline
discuss
disgust
dish
dismiss
disturb
ditch
dive
dollar
donkey
dot
dozen
drag
drawer
drink
drown
drum
duck
dull
dust
duty
eager
earn
earnest
ease
educate
efficient
egg
elastic
elder
elect
electricity
elephant
empire
empty
enclose
encourage
engine
entertain
envelope
envy
especial
essence
exact
examination
excess
excite

excuse
explode
explore
extra
extraordinary
extreme
fade
faint
false
fan
fancy
far
farther
fat
fate
fault
feast
feather
female
fence
fever
fierce
fight
film
firm
flag
flame
flash
flat
flavour
flesh
float
flood
flour
flow
fly
fold
fond
fool
foot
forbid
forest
forgive
fork
formal
frame
freeze
frequent
fresh
fright
fruit
fry
fun
funeral
fur
furnish
gallon
gap
garage
gas
gay
generous
girl
glory
goat
govern
grace
gradual
grain
grammar
grand
grass
grateful
grave
grease
greed
greet
grey
grind
guess
guest
guide
guilty
gun
hair
hammer
handkerchief
harbour
harm
harvest
haste
hat
hate
hay
heal
heap
heart
height
hesitate
hinder
hire
hit
hole
holiday
hollow
holy
honest
hook
horizon
hospital
host
hotel
humble
hunger
hunt
hurry
hurt

hut
ice
ideal
idle
ill
imagine
imitate
immediate
immense
important
improve
indoors
industry
inform
ink
in-law
inn
inquire
insect
inside
instant
instrument
insult
insure
interfere
international
interrupt
invent
invite
inward/s
island
jaw
jealous
jewel
joint
joke
journey
joy
juice
jump
key
kick
king
kiss
kitchen
knee
kneel
knife
knock
knot
ladder
lake
lamp
latter
laugh
lazy
leaf
lean
leather
leg
lend
lessen
lesson
liberty
lid
limb
lip
liquid
list
literature
load
loaf
loan
lock
lodging
log
lonely
loose
lord
loud
loyal
luck
lump
lunch
lung
mad
mail
male
manage
manufacture
map
master
mat
match
meal
meanwhile
meat
mechanic
medicine
melt
mend
merchant
mercy
merry
message
mild
milk
mill
miserable
mistake
mix
model
moderate
modest
monkey
moon
moral

motion
mouse
mud
multiply
murder
mystery
nail
neat
needle
neglect
nephew
nest
net
nice
niece
noble
noise
nonsense
noon
nose
noun
nuisance
nurse
nut
oar
obey
ocean
offend
omit
onto
opposite
orange
organ
origin
ornament
overcome
pack
pad
pair
pale
pan
parcel
pardon
parent
park
particular
passage
paste
path
patient
pattern
pause
paw
pearl
peculiar
pen
pencil
penny
per
perform
persuade
pet
photograph
pick
pig
pigeon
pile
pin
pinch
pink
pint
pipe
pity
plain
plaster
plate
plenty
plough
plural
pocket
poet
poison
police
polish
polite
pool
postpone
pot
pour
powder
practice
praise
pray
preach
precious
prefer
prejudice
president
pretend
pride
priest
prison
prize
probable
procession
profession
profit
prompt
pronounce
property
proud
pump
punctual
punish
pupil
pure
purple

push
puzzle
qualify
quantity
quarrel
quart
queen
question
quick
rabbit
radio
rail
rain
rake
rapid
rare
rat
raw
ray
razor
recommend
refer
reflect
refresh
regret
rejoice
relieve
remedy
remind
rent
repair
replace
reproduce
republic
reputation
request
rescue
reserve
resign
resist
responsible
restaurant
retire
revenge
review
reward
ribbon
rice
rid
ripe
risk
rival
roar
roast
rob
rock
rod
roof
root
rope
rot
row
royal
rub
rubber
rubbish
rude
rug
ruin
rust
sacred
sacrifice
sad
saddle
sake
salary
sale
salt
sample
sand
satisfy
sauce
saucer
scatter
scent
scissors
scold
scorn
scrape
scratch
screen
screw
search
seed
seldom
sentence
severe
sew
shade
shallow
shame
sharp
sheep
sheet
shelf
shell
shelter
shield
shilling
ship
shirt
shock
shop
shout
shower
shut
sick

signal
silk
sincere
sing
sink
skin
skirt
slave
slide
slip
slope
smell
smoke
smooth
snake
snow
soap
socks
soldier
solemn
solid
solve
sore
sorry
soul
soup
sour
sow
spade
spare
spell
spill
spin
spit
splendid
split
spoil
spoon
sport
staff
stain
stairs
stamp
star
steady
steam
steep
steer
stem
stiff
sting
stir
stockings
stomach
stove
strap
straw
strict
string
strip
stripe
stuff
stupid
suck
sugar
suit
supper
suspect
swallow
swear
sweat
sweep
swell
swim
swing
sword
sympathy
tail
tailor
tall
tame
tap
tax
taxi
tea
telegraph
telephone
temper
temperature
temple
tempt
tend
tender
tent
thank/s
theatre
thick
thief
thin
thirst
thorn
thorough
thread
threaten
throat
thumb
thunder
ticket
tide
tidy
tie
tight
till
tin
tip
tire
title

| | | |
|---|---|---|
| tobacco | ugly | weapon |
| toe | umbrella | weather |
| tomorrow | uncle | weave |
| ton | unit | weed |
| tongue | unity | weigh |
| tonight | universe | wet |
| tool | upper | wheat |
| tooth | upright | wheel |
| tough | upset | whip |
| tour | upwards | whisper |
| towel | urge | whistle |
| tower | vain | whole |
| toy | veil | wicked |
| track | verb | widow |
| translate | verse | wine |
| trap | vessel | wipe |
| tray | victory | wire |
| treasure | violent | witness |
| treat | virtue | wool |
| tremble | vowel | worm |
| trial | voyage | worry |
| tribe | wage/ s | worship |
| trick | waist | wound |
| trip | wake | wrap |
| true | wander | wreck |
| trunk | warm | wrist |
| tube | wash | yard |
| tune | wax | yield |
| twist | wealth | zero |

# Appendix 15. Headwords of the Academic Word List

This list contains the headwords of the word families appearing in the Academic Word List (Coxhead 1998: 114–118).

abandon
abstract
academy
access
accommodate
accompany
accumulate
accurate
achieve
acknowledge
acquire
adapt
adequate
adjacent
adjust
administrate
adult
advocate
affect
aggregate
aid
albeit
allocate
alter
alternative
ambiguous
amend
analogy
analyse
annual
anticipate
apparent
append
appreciate
approach
appropriate
approximate
arbitrary
area
aspect
assemble
assess
assign
assist
assume
assure
attach
attain
attitude
attribute
author
authority
automate
available
aware
behalf
benefit
bias
bond
brief
bulk
capable
capacity
category
cease
challenge
channel
chapter
chart

chemical
circumstance
cite
civil
clarify
classic
clause
code
coherent
coincide
collapse
colleague
commence
comment
commission
commit
commodity
communicate
community
compatible
compensate
compile
complement
complex
component
compound
comprehensive
comprise
compute
conceive
concentrate
concept
conclude
concurrent
conduct
confer
confine
confirm
conflict
conform
consent
consequent
considerable
consist
constant
constitute
constrain
construct
consult
consume
contact
contemporary
context
contract
contradict
contrary
contrast
contribute
controversy
convene
converse
convert
convince
cooperate
coordinate
core
corporate
correspond
couple
create
credit
criteria
crucial
culture
currency
cycle
data
debate
decade
decline
deduce
define
definite
demonstrate
denote
deny
depress
derive
design
despite
detect
deviate
device
devote
differentiate
dimension
diminish
discrete
discriminate
displace
display
dispose
distinct
distort
distribute
diverse
document
domain
domestic
dominate
draft
drama
duration
dynamic
economy
edit
element

eliminate
emerge
emphasis
empirical
enable
encounter
energy
enforce
enhance
enormous
ensure
entity
environment
equate
equip
equivalent
erode
error
establish
estate
estimate
ethic
ethnic
evaluate
eventual
evident
evolve
exceed
exclude
exhibit
expand
expert
explicit
exploit
export
expose
external
extract
facilitate
factor
feature
federal
fee
file
final
finance
finite
flexible
fluctuate
focus
format
formula
forthcoming
foundation
found
framework
function
fund
fundamental
furthermore
gender
generate
generation
globe
goal
grade
grant
guarantee
guideline
hence
hierarchy
highlight
hypothesis
identical
identify
ideology
ignorance
illustrate
image
immigrate
impact
implement
implicate
implicit
imply
impose
incentive
incidence
incline
income
incorporate
index
indicate
individual
induce
inevitable
infer
infrastructure
inherent
inhibit
initial
initiate
injure
innovate
input
insert
insight
inspect
instance
institute
instruct
integral
integrate
integrity
intelligence
intense
interact

intermediate
internal
interpret
interval
intervene
intrinsic
invest
investigate
invoke
involve
isolate
issue
item
job
journal
justify
label
labour
layer
lecture
legal
legislate
levy
liberal
licence
likewise
link
locate
logic
maintain
major
manipulate
manual
margin
mature
maximise
mechanism
media
mediate
medical
medium
mental
method
migrate
military
minimal
minimise
minimum
ministry
minor
mode
modify
monitor
motive
mutual
negate
network
neutral
nevertheless
nonetheless
norm
normal
notion
notwithstanding
nuclear
objective
obtain
obvious
occupy
occur
odd
offset
ongoing
option
orient
outcome
output
overall
overlap
overseas
panel
paradigm
paragraph
parallel
parameter
participate
partner
passive
perceive
percent
period
persist
perspective
phase
phenomenon
philosophy
physical
plus
policy
portion
pose
positive
potential
practitioner
precede
precise
predict
predominant
preliminary
presume
previous
primary
prime
principal
principle
prior
priority

proceed
process
professional
prohibit
project
promote
proportion
prospect
protocol
psychology
publication
publish
purchase
pursue
qualitative
quote
radical
random
range
ratio
rational
react
recover
refine
regime
region
register
regulate
reinforce
reject
relax
release
relevant
reluctance
rely
remove
require
research
reside

resolve
resource
respond
restore
restrain
restrict
retain
reveal
revenue
reverse
revise
revolution
rigid
role
route
scenario
schedule
scheme
scope
section
sector
secure
seek
select
sequence
series
sex
shift
significant
similar
simulate
site
so-called
sole
somewhat
source
specific
specify
sphere

stable
statistic
status
straightforward
strategy
stress
structure
style
submit
subordinate
subsequent
subsidy
substitute
successor
sufficient
sum
summary
supplement
survey
survive
suspend
sustain
symbol
tape
target
task
team
technical
technique
technology
temporary
tense
terminate
text
theme
theory
thereby
thesis
topic

trace
tradition
transfer
transform
transit
transmit
transport
trend
trigger
ultimate
undergo
underlie
undertake
uniform
unify
unique
utilise
valid
vary
vehicle
version
via
violate
virtual
visible
vision
visual
volume
voluntary
welfare
whereas
whereby
widespread

# Index

# Linguistic Insights

Studies in Language and Communication

This series aims to promote specialist language studies in the fields of linguistic theory and applied linguistics, by publishing volumes that focus on specific aspects of language use in one or several languages and provide valuable insights into language and communication research. A cross-disciplinary approach is favoured and most European languages are accepted.

The series includes two types of books:

- Monographs – featuring in- depth studies on special aspects of language theory, language analysis or language teaching.
- Collected papers – assembling papers from workshops, conferences or symposia.

Each volume of the series is subjected to a double peer-reviewing process.

Vol. 1 Maurizio Gotti & Marina Dossena (eds)
Modality in Specialized Texts. Selected Papers of the 1st CERLIS Conference.
421 pages. 2001. ISBN 3-906767-10-8 · US-ISBN 0-8204-5340-4

Vol. 2 Giuseppina Cortese & Philip Riley (eds)
Domain-specific English. Textual Practices across Communities and Classrooms.
420 pages. 2002. ISBN 3-906768-98-8 · US-ISBN 0-8204-5884-8

Vol. 3 Maurizio Gotti, Dorothee Heller & Marina Dossena (eds)
Conflict and Negotiation in Specialized Texts. Selected Papers of the 2nd CERLIS Conference.
470 pages. 2002. ISBN 3-906769-12-7 · US-ISBN 0-8204-5887-2

Vol. 4 Maurizio Gotti, Marina Dossena, Richard Dury, Roberta Facchinetti & Maria Lima
Variation in Central Modals. A Repertoire of Forms and Types of Usage in Middle English and Early Modern English.
364 pages. 2002. ISBN 3-906769-84-4 · US-ISBN 0-8204-5898-8

***Editorial address:***

Prof. Maurizio Gotti Università di Bergamo, Dipartimento di Lingue, Letterature e Culture Straniere Piazza Rosate 2, 24129 Bergamo, Italy
Fax: + 39 035 2052789, E-Mail: m.gotti@unibg.it

Vol. 5 Stefania Nuccorini (ed.)
Phrases and Phraseology. Data and Descriptions.
187 pages. 2002. ISBN 3-906770-08-7 · US-ISBN 0-8204-5933-X

Vol. 6 Vijay Bhatia, Christopher N. Candlin & Maurizio Gotti (eds)
Legal Discourse in Multilingual and Multicultural Contexts. Arbitration Texts in Europe.
385 pages. 2003. ISBN 3-906770-85-0 · US-ISBN 0-8204-6254-3

Vol. 7 Marina Dossena & Charles Jones (eds)
Insights into Late Modern English. 2nd edition.
378 pages. 2003, 2007. ISBN 978-3-03911-257-9 ·
US-ISBN 978-0-8204-8927-8

Vol. 8 Maurizio Gotti
Specialized Discourse. Linguistic Features and Changing Conventions.
351 pages. 2003, 2005.
ISBN 3-03910-606-6 · US-ISBN 0-8204-7000-7

Vol. 9 Alan Partington, John Morley & Louann Haarman (eds)
Corpora and Discourse.
420 pages. 2004. ISBN 3-03910-026-2 · US-ISBN 0-8204-6262-4

Vol. 10 Martina Möllering
The Acquisition of German Modal Particles. A Corpus-Based Approach.
290 pages. 2004. ISBN 3-03910-043-2 · US-ISBN 0-8204-6273-X

Vol. 11 David Hart (ed.)
English Modality in Context. Diachronic Perspectives.
261 pages. 2003. ISBN 3-03910-046-7 · US-ISBN 0-8204-6852-5

Vol. 12 Wendy Swanson
Modes of Co-reference as an Indicator of Genre.
430 pages. 2003. ISBN 3-03910-052-1 · US-ISBN 0-8204-6855-X

Vol. 13 Gina Poncini
Discursive Strategies in Multicultural Business Meetings. 2nd edition.
338 pages. 2004, 2007. ISBN 978-3-03911-296-8 · US-ISBN 978-0-8204-8937-7

Vol. 14 Christopher N. Candlin & Maurizio Gotti (eds)
Intercultural Aspects of Specialized Communication. 2nd edition.
369 pages. 2004, 2007. ISBN 978-3-03911-258-6 · US-ISBN 978-0-8204-8926-1

Vol. 15 Gabriella Del Lungo Camiciotti & Elena Tognini Bonelli (eds)
Academic Discourse. New Insights into Evaluation.
234 pages. 2004. ISBN 3-03910-353-9 · US-ISBN 0-8204-7016-3

Vol. 16 Marina Dossena & Roger Lass (eds)
Methods and Data in English Historical Dialectology.
405 pages. 2004. ISBN 3-03910-362-8 · US-ISBN 0-8204-7018-X

Vol. 17 Judy Noguchi
The Science Review Article. An Opportune Genre in the Construction of Science.
274 pages. 2006. ISBN 3-03910-426-8 · US-ISBN 0-8204-7034-1

Vol. 18 Giuseppina Cortese & Anna Duszak (eds)
Identity, Community, Discourse. English in Intercultural Settings.
495 pages. 2005. ISBN 3-03910-632-5 · US-ISBN 0-8204-7163-1

Vol. 19 Anna Trosborg & Poul Erik Flyvholm Jørgensen (eds)
Business Discourse. Texts and Contexts.
250 pages. 2005. ISBN 3-03910-606-6 · US-ISBN 0-8204-7000-7

Vol. 20 Christopher Williams
Tradition and Change in Legal English. Verbal Constructions in Prescriptive Texts.
2nd revised edition.
216 pages. 2005, 2007. ISBN 978-3-03911-444-3.

Vol. 21 Katarzyna Dziubalska-Kolaczyk & Joanna Przedlacka (eds)
English Pronunciation Models: A Changing Scene.
2nd edition. 476 pages. 2005, 2008. ISBN 978-3-03911-682-9.

Vol. 22 Christián Abello-Contesse, Rubén Chacón-Beltrán, M. Dolores López-Jiménez & M. Mar Torreblanca-López (eds)
Age in L2 Acquisition and Teaching.
214 pages. 2006. ISBN 3-03910-668-6 · US-ISBN 0-8204-7174-7

Vol. 23 Vijay K. Bhatia, Maurizio Gotti, Jan Engberg & Dorothee Heller (eds)
Vagueness in Normative Texts.
474 pages. 2005. ISBN 3-03910-653-8 · US-ISBN 0-8204-7169-0

Vol. 24 Paul Gillaerts & Maurizio Gotti (eds)
Genre Variation in Business Letters. 2nd printing.
407 pages. 2008. ISBN 978-3-03911-681-2.

Vol. 25 Ana María Hornero, María José Luzón & Silvia Murillo (eds)
Corpus Linguistics. Applications for the Study of English. 2nd printing.
526 pages. 2006, 2008. ISBN 978-3-03911-726-0

Vol. 26 J. Lachlan Mackenzie & María de los Ángeles Gómez-González (eds)
Studies in Functional Discourse Grammar.
259 pages. 2005. ISBN 3-03910-696-1 · US-ISBN 0-8204-7558-0

Vol. 27 Debbie G. E. Ho
Classroom Talk. Exploring the Sociocultural Structure of Formal ESL Learning. 2nd edition.
254 pages. 2006, 2007. ISBN 978-3-03911-434-4

Vol. 28 Javier Pérez-Guerra, Dolores González-Álvarez, Jorge L. Bueno-Alonso & Esperanza Rama-Martínez (eds)
'Of Varying Language and Opposing Creed'. New Insights into Late Modern English.
455 pages. 2007. ISBN 978-3-03910-788-9

Vol. 29 Francesca Bargiela-Chiappini & Maurizio Gotti (eds)
Asian Business Discourse(s).
350 pages. 2005. ISBN 3-03910-804-2 · US-ISBN 0-8204-7574-2

Vol. 30 Nicholas Brownlees (ed.)
News Discourse in Early Modern Britain. Selected Papers of CHINED 2004.
300 pages. 2006. ISBN 3-03910-805-0 · US-ISBN 0-8204-8025-8

Vol. 31 Roberta Facchinetti & Matti Rissanen (eds)
Corpus-based Studies of Diachronic English.
300 pages. 2006. ISBN 3-03910-851-4 · US-ISBN 0-8204-8040-1

Vol. 32 Marina Dossena & Susan M. Fitzmaurice (eds)
Business and Official Correspondence. Historical Investigations.
209 pages. 2006. ISBN 3-03910-880-8 · US-ISBN 0-8204-8352-4

Vol. 33 Giuliana Garzone & Srikant Sarangi (eds)
Discourse, Ideology and Specialized Communication.
494 pages. 2007. ISBN 978-3-03910-888-6

Vol. 34 Giuliana Garzone & Cornelia Ilie (eds)
The Use of English in Institutional and Business Settings. An Intercultural Perspective.
372 pages. 2007. ISBN 978-3-03910-889-3

Vol. 35 Vijay K. Bhatia & Maurizio Gotti (eds)
Explorations in Specialized Genres.
316 pages. 2006. ISBN 3-03910-995-2 · US-ISBN 0-8204-8372-9

Vol. 36 Heribert Picht (ed.)
Modern Approaches to Terminological Theories and Applications.
432 pages. 2006. ISBN 3-03911-156-6 · US-ISBN 0-8204-8380-X

Vol. 37 Anne Wagner & Sophie Cacciaguidi-Fahy (eds)
Legal Language and the Search for Clarity / Le langage juridique et la quête de clarté.
Practice and Tools / Pratiques et instruments.
487 pages. 2006. ISBN 3-03911-169-8 · US-ISBN 0-8204-8388-5

Vol. 38 Juan Carlos Palmer-Silveira, Miguel F. Ruiz-Garrido & Inmaculada Fortanet-Gómez (eds)
Intercultural and International Business Communication. Theory, Research and Teaching. 2nd edition.
343 pages. 2006, 2008. ISBN 978-3-03911-680-5

Vol. 39 Christiane Dalton-Puffer, Dieter Kastovsky, Nikolaus Ritt & Herbert Schendl (eds)
Syntax, Style and Grammatical Norms. English from 1500–2000.
250 pages. 2006. ISBN 3-03911-181-7 · US-ISBN 0-8204-8394-X

Vol. 40 Marina Dossena & Irma Taavitsainen (eds)
Diachronic Perspectives on Domain-Specific English.
280 pages. 2006. ISBN 3-03910-176-0 · US-ISBN 0-8204-8391-5

Vol. 41 John Flowerdew & Maurizio Gotti (eds)
Studies in Specialized Discourse.
293 pages. 2006. ISBN 3-03911-178-7

Vol. 42 Ken Hyland & Marina Bondi (eds)
Academic Discourse Across Disciplines.
320 pages. 2006. ISBN 3-03911-183-3 · US-ISBN 0-8204-8396-6

Vol. 43 Paul Gillaerts & Philip Shaw (eds)
The Map and the Landscape. Norms and Practices in Genre.
256 pages. 2006. ISBN 3-03911-182-5 · US-ISBN 0-8204-8395-4

Vol. 44 Maurizio Gotti & Davide Giannoni (eds)
New Trends in Specialized Discourse Analysis.
301 pages. 2006. ISBN 3-03911-184-1 · US-ISBN 0-8204-8381-8

Vol. 45 Maurizio Gotti & Françoise Salager-Meyer (eds)
Advances in Medical Discourse Analysis. Oral and Written Contexts.
492 pages. 2006. ISBN 3-03911-185-X · US-ISBN 0-8204-8382-6

Vol. 46 Maurizio Gotti & Susan Šarcević (eds)
Insights into Specialized Translation.
396 pages. 2006. ISBN 3-03911-186-8 · US-ISBN 0-8204-8383-4

Vol. 47 Khurshid Ahmad & Margaret Rogers (eds)
Evidence-based LSP. Translation, Text and Terminology.
584 pages. 2007. ISBN 978-3-03911-187-9

Vol. 48 Hao Sun & Dániel Z. Kádár (eds)
It's the Dragon's Turn. Chinese Institutional Discourses.
262 pages. 2008. ISBN 978-3-03911-175-6

Vol. 49 Cristina Suárez-Gómez
Relativization in Early English (950-1250): the Position of Relative Clauses.
149 pages. 2006. ISBN 3-03911-203-1 · US-ISBN 0-8204-8904-2

Vol. 50 Maria Vittoria Calvi & Luisa Chierichetti (eds)
Nuevas tendencias en el discurso de especialidad
319 pages. 2006. ISBN 978- 3- 03911- 261- 6

Vol. 51 Mari Carmen Campoy & María José Luzón (eds)
Spoken Corpora in Applied Linguistics.
274 pages. 2008. ISBN 978-3-03911-275-3

Vol. 52 Konrad Ehlich & Dorothee Heller (Hrsg.)
Die Wissenschaft und ihre Sprachen.
323 pages. 2006. ISBN 978-3-03911-272-2

Vol. 53 Jingyu Zhang
The Semantic Salience Hierarchy Model. The L2 Acquisition of Psych Predicates.
273 pages. 2007. ISBN 978-3-03911-300-2

Vol. 54 Norman Fairclough, Giuseppina Cortese & Patrizia Ardizzone (eds)
Discourse and Contemporary Social Change.
555 pages. 2007. ISBN 978-3-03911-276-0

Vol. 55 Jan Engberg, Marianne Grove Ditlevsen, Peter Kastberg & Martin Stegu (eds)
New Directions in LSP Teaching.
331 pages. 2007. ISBN 978-3-03911-433-7

Vol. 56 Dorothee Heller & Konrad Ehlich (Hrsg.)
Studien zur Rechtskommunikation.
322 pages. 2007. ISBN 978-3-03911-436-8

Vol. 57 Teruhiro Ishiguro & Kang-kwong Luke (eds)
Grammar in Cross-Linguistic Perspective. The Syntax, Semantics, and Pragmatics of Japanese and Chinese.
304 pages. 2012. ISBN 978-3-03911-445-0

Vol. 58 Carmen Frehner
Email – SMS – MMS.
294 pages. 2008. ISBN 978-3-03911-451-1

Vol. 59 Isabel Balteiro
The Directionality of Conversion in English. A Dia-Synchronic Study.
276 pages. 2007. ISBN 978-3-03911-241-8

Vol. 60 Maria Milagros Del Saz Rubio
English Discourse Markers of Reformulation.
237 pages. 2007. ISBN 978-3-03911-196-1

Vol. 61 Sally Burgess & Pedro Martín-Martín (eds)
English as an Additional Language in Research Publication and Communication.
259 pages. 2008. ISBN 978-3-03911-462-7

Vol. 62 Sandrine Onillon
Pratiques et représentations de l'écrit.
458 pages. 2008. ISBN 978-3-03911-464-1

Vol. 63 Hugo Bowles & Paul Seedhouse (eds)
Conversation Analysis and Language for Specific Purposes.
2nd edition. 337 pages. 2007, 2009. ISBN 978-3-0343-0045-2

Vol. 64 Vijay K. Bhatia, Christopher N. Candlin & Paola Evangelisti Allori (eds)
Language, Culture and the Law. The Formulation of Legal Concepts across Systems and Cultures.
342 pages. 2008. ISBN 978-3-03911-470-2

Vol. 65 Jonathan Culpeper & Dániel Z. Kádár (eds)
Historical (Im)politeness.
300 pages. 2010. ISBN 978-3-03911-496-2

Vol. 66 Linda Lombardo (ed.)
Using Corpora to Learn about Language and Discourse.
237 pages. 2009. ISBN 978-3-03911-522-8

Vol. 67 Natsumi Wakamoto
Extroversion/Introversion in Foreign Language Learning. Interactions with Learner Strategy Use.
159 pages. 2009. ISBN 978-3-03911-596-9

Vol. 68 Eva Alcón-Soler (ed.)
Learning How to Request in an Instructed Language Learning Context.
260 pages. 2008. ISBN 978-3-03911-601-0

Vol. 69 Domenico Pezzini
The Translation of Religious Texts in the Middle Ages.
428 pages. 2008. ISBN 978-3-03911-600-3

Vol. 70 Tomoko Tode
Effects of Frequency in Classroom Second Language Learning. Quasi-experiment and stimulated-recall analysis.
195 pages. 2008. ISBN 978-3-03911-602-7

Vol. 71 Egor Tsedryk
Fusion symétrique et alternances ditransitives.
211 pages. 2009. ISBN 978-3-03911-609-6

Vol. 72 Cynthia J. Kellett Bidoli & Elana Ochse (eds)
English in International Deaf Communication.
444 pages. 2008. ISBN 978-3-03911-610-2

Vol. 73 Joan C. Beal, Carmela Nocera & Massimo Sturiale (eds)
Perspectives on Prescriptivism.
269 pages. 2008. ISBN 978-3-03911-632-4

Vol. 74 Carol Taylor Torsello, Katherine Ackerley & Erik Castello (eds)
Corpora for University Language Teachers.
308 pages. 2008. ISBN 978-3-03911-639-3

Vol. 75 María Luisa Pérez Cañado (ed.)
English Language Teaching in the European Credit Transfer System. Facing the Challenge.
251 pages. 2009. ISBN 978-3-03911-654-6

Vol. 76 Marina Dossena & Ingrid Tieken-Boon van Ostade (eds)
Studies in Late Modern English Correspondence. Methodology and Data.
291 pages. 2008. ISBN 978-3-03911-658-4

Vol. 77 Ingrid Tieken-Boon van Ostade & Wim van der Wurff (eds)
Current Issues in Late Modern English.
436 pages. 2009. ISBN 978-3-03911-660-7

Vol. 78 Marta Navarro Coy (ed.)
Practical Approaches to Foreign Language Teaching and Learning.
297 pages. 2009. ISBN 978-3-03911-661-4

Vol. 79 Qing Ma
Second Language Vocabulary Acquisition.
333 pages. 2009. ISBN 978-3-03911-666-9

Vol. 80 Martin Solly, Michelangelo Conoscenti & Sandra Campagna (eds)
Verbal/Visual Narrative Texts in Higher Education.
384 pages. 2008. ISBN 978-3-03911-672-0

Vol. 81 Meiko Matsumoto
From Simple Verbs to Periphrastic Expressions: The Historical Development of Composite Predicates, Phrasal Verbs, and Related Constructions in English.
235 pages. 2008. ISBN 978-3-03911-675-1

Vol. 82 Melinda Dooly
Doing Diversity. Teachers' Construction of Their Classroom Reality.
180 pages. 2009. ISBN 978-3-03911-687-4

Vol. 83 Victoria Guillén-Nieto, Carmen Marimón-Llorca & Chelo Vargas-Sierra (eds)
Intercultural Business Communication and Simulation and Gaming Methodology.
392 pages. 2009. ISBN 978-3-03911-688-1

Vol. 84 Maria Grazia Guido
English as a Lingua Franca in Cross-cultural Immigration Domains.
285 pages. 2008. ISBN 978-3-03911-689-8

Vol. 85 Erik Castello
Text Complexity and Reading Comprehension Tests.
352 pages. 2008. ISBN 978-3-03911-717-8

Vol. 86 Maria-Lluisa Gea-Valor, Isabel García-Izquierdo & Maria-José Esteve (eds)
Linguistic and Translation Studies in Scientific Communication.
317 pages. 2010. ISBN 978-3-0343-0069-8

Vol. 87 Carmen Navarro, Rosa Ma Rodríguez Abella, Francesca Dalle Pezze & Renzo Miotti (eds)
La comunicación especializada.
355 pages. 2008. ISBN 978-3-03911-733-8

Vol. 88 Kiriko Sato
The Development from Case-Forms to Prepositional Constructions in Old English Prose.
231 pages. 2009. ISBN 978-3-03911-763-5

Vol. 89 Dorothee Heller (Hrsg.)
Formulierungsmuster in deutscher und italienischer Fachkommunikation. Intra- und interlinguale Perspektiven.
315 pages. 2008. ISBN 978-3-03911-778-9

Vol. 90 Henning Bergenholtz, Sandro Nielsen & Sven Tarp (eds)
Lexicography at a Crossroads. Dictionaries and Encyclopedias Today, Lexicographical Tools Tomorrow.
372 pages. 2009. ISBN 978-3-03911-799-4

Vol. 91 Manouchehr Moshtagh Khorasani
The Development of Controversies. From the Early Modern Period to Online Discussion Forums.
317 pages. 2009. ISBN 978-3-3911-711-6

Vol. 92 María Luisa Carrió-Pastor (ed.)
Content and Language Integrated Learning. Cultural Diversity.
178 pages. 2009. ISBN 978-3-3911-818-2

Vol. 93 Roger Berry
Terminology in English Language Teaching. Nature and Use.
262 pages. 2010. ISBN 978-3-0343-0013-1

Vol. 94 Roberto Cagliero & Jennifer Jenkins (eds)
Discourses, Communities, and Global Englishes.
240 pages. 2010. ISBN 978-3-0343-0012-4

Vol. 95 Facchinetti Roberta, Crystal David, Seidlhofer Barbara (eds)
From International to Local English – And Back Again.
268 pages. 2010. ISBN 978-3-0343-0011-7

Vol. 96 Cesare Gagliardi & Alan Maley (eds)
EIL, ELF, Global English. Teaching and Learning Issues.
376 pages. 2010. ISBN 978-3-0343-0010-0

Vol. 97 Sylvie Hancil (ed.)
The Role of Prosody in Affective Speech.
403 pages. 2009. ISBN 978-3-03911-696-6

Vol. 98 Marina Dossena & Roger Lass (eds)
Studies in English and European Historical Dialectology.
257 pages. 2009. ISBN 978-3-0343-0024-7

Vol. 99 Christine Béal
Les interactions quotidiennes en français et en anglais. De l'approche comparative à l'analyse des situations interculturelles.
424 pages. 2010. ISBN 978-3-0343-0027-8

Vol. 100 Maurizio Gotti (ed.)
Commonality and Individuality in Academic Discourse.
398 pages. 2009. ISBN 978-3-0343-0023-0

Vol. 101 Javier E. Díaz Vera & Rosario Caballero (eds)
Textual Healing. Studies in Medieval English Medical, Scientific and Technical Texts.
213 pages. 2009. ISBN 978-3-03911-822-9

Vol. 102 Nuria Edo Marzá
The Specialised Lexicographical Approach. A Step further in Dictionary-making.
316 pages. 2009. ISBN 978-3-0343-0043-8

Vol. 103 Carlos Prado-Alonso, Lidia Gómez-García, Iria Pastor-Gómez & David Tizón-Couto (eds)
New Trends and Methodologies in Applied English Language Research. Diachronic, Diatopic and Contrastive Studies.
348 pages. 2009. ISBN 978-3-0343-0046-9

Vol. 104 Françoise Salager-Meyer & Beverly A. Lewin
Crossed Words. Criticism in Scholarly Writing?
371 pages. 2011. ISBN 978-3-0343-0049-0.

Vol. 105 Javier Ruano-García
Early Modern Northern English Lexis. A Literary Corpus-Based Study.
611 pages. 2010. ISBN 978-3-0343-0058-2

Vol. 106 Rafael Monroy-Casas
Systems for the Phonetic Transcription of English. Theory and Texts.
280 pages. 2011. ISBN 978-3-0343-0059-9

Vol. 107 Nicola T. Owtram
The Pragmatics of Academic Writing. A Relevance Approach to the Analysis of Research Article Introductions.
311 pages. 2009. ISBN 978-3-0343-0060-5

Vol. 108 Yolanda Ruiz de Zarobe, Juan Manuel Sierra & Francisco Gallardo del Puerto (eds)
Content and Foreign Language Integrated Learning. Contributions to Multilingualism in European Contexts.
343 pages. 2011. ISBN 978-3-0343-0074-2

Vol. 109 Ángeles Linde López & Rosalía Crespo Jiménez (eds)
Professional English in the European context. The EHEA challenge.
374 pages. 2010. ISBN 978-3-0343-0088-9

Vol. 110 Rosalía Rodríguez-Vázquez
The Rhythm of Speech, Verse and Vocal Music. A New Theory.
394 pages. 2010. ISBN 978-3-0343-0309-5

Vol. 111 Anastasios Tsangalidis & Roberta Facchinetti (eds)
Studies on English Modality. In Honour of Frank Palmer.
392 pages. 2009. ISBN 978-3-0343-0310-1

Vol. 112 Jing Huang
Autonomy, Agency and Identity in Foreign Language Learning and Teaching.
400 pages. 2013. ISBN 978-3-0343-0370-5

Vol. 113 Mihhail Lotman & Maria-Kristiina Lotman (eds)
Frontiers in Comparative Prosody. In memoriam: Mikhail Gasparov.
426 pages. 2011. ISBN 978-3-0343-0373-6

Vol. 114 Merja Kytö, John Scahill & Harumi Tanabe (eds)
Language Change and Variation from Old English to Late Modern English. A Festschrift for Minoji Akimoto.
422 pages. 2010. ISBN 978-3-0343-0372-9

Vol. 115 Giuliana Garzone & Paola Catenaccio (eds)
Identities across Media and Modes. Discursive Perspectives.
379 pages. 2009. ISBN 978-3-0343-0386-6

Vol. 116 Elena Landone
Los marcadores del discurso y cortesía verbal en español.
390 pages. 2010. ISBN 978-3-0343-0413-9

Vol. 117 Maurizio Gotti & Christopher Williams (eds)
Legal Discourse across Languages and Cultures.
339 pages. 2010. ISBN 978-3-0343-0425-2

Vol. 118 David Hirsh
Academic Vocabulary in Context.
217 pages. 2010. ISBN 978-3-0343-0426-9

Vol. 119 Yvonne Dröschel
Lingua Franca English. The Role of Simplification and Transfer.
358 pages. 2011. ISBN 978-3-0343-0432-0

Vol. 120 Tengku Sepora Tengku Mahadi, Helia Vaezian & Mahmoud Akbari
Corpora in Translation. A Practical Guide.
135 pages. 2010. ISBN 978-3-0343-0434-4

Vol. 121 Davide Simone Giannoni & Celina Frade (eds)
Researching Language and the Law. Textual Features and Translation Issues.
278 pages. 2010. ISBN 978-3-0343-0443-6

Vol. 122 Daniel Madrid & Stephen Hughes (eds)
Studies in Bilingual Education.
472 pages. 2011. ISBN 978-3-0343-0474-0

Vol. 123 Vijay K. Bhatia, Christopher N. Candlin & Maurizio Gotti (eds)
The Discourses of Dispute Resolution.
290 pages. 2010. ISBN 978-3-0343-0476-4

Vol. 124 Davide Simone Giannoni
Mapping Academic Values in the Disciplines. A Corpus-Based Approach.
288 pages. 2010. ISBN 978-3-0343-0488-7

Vol. 125 Giuliana Garzone & James Archibald (eds)
Discourse, Identities and Roles in Specialized Communication.
419 pages. 2010. ISBN 978-3-0343-0494-8

Vol. 126 Iria Pastor-Gómez
The Status and Development of N+N Sequences in Contemporary English Noun Phrases.
216 pages. 2011. ISBN 978-3-0343-0534-1

Vol. 127 Carlos Prado-Alonso
Full-verb Inversion in Written and Spoken English.
261 pages. 2011. ISBN 978-3-0343-0535-8

Vol. 128 Tony Harris & María Moreno Jaén (eds)
Corpus Linguistics in Language Teaching.
214 pages. 2010. ISBN 978-3-0343-0524-2

Vol. 129 Tetsuji Oda & Hiroyuki Eto (eds)
Multiple Perspectives on English Philology and History of Linguistics. A Festschrift for Shoichi Watanabe on his 80th Birthday.
378 pages. 2010. ISBN 978-3-0343-0480-1

Vol. 130 Luisa Chierichetti & Giovanni Garofalo (eds)
Lengua y Derecho. líneas de investigación interdisciplinaria.
283 pages. 2010. 978-3-0343-0463-4

Vol. 131 Paola Evangelisti Allori & Giuliana Garzone (eds)
Discourse, Identities and Genres in Corporate Communication. Sponsorship, Advertising and Organizational Communication.
324 pages. 2011. 978-3-0343-0591-4

Vol. 132 Leyre Ruiz de Zarobe & Yolanda Ruiz de Zarobe (eds)
Speech Acts and Politeness across Languages and Cultures.
402 pages. 2012. 978-3-0343-0611-9

Vol. 133 Thomas Christiansen
Cohesion. A Discourse Perspective.
387 pages. 2011. 978-3-0343-0619-5

Vol. 134 Giuliana Garzone & Maurizio Gotti
Discourse, Communication and the Enterprise. Genres and Trends.
451 pages. 2011. ISBN 978-3-0343-0620-1

Vol. 135 Zsuzsa Hoffmann
Ways of the World's Words. Language Contact in the Age of Globalization.
334 pages 2011. ISBN 978-3-0343-0673-7

Vol. 136 Cecilia Varcasia (ed.)
Becoming Multilingual. Language Learning and Language Policy between Attitudes and Identities.
213 pages. 2011. ISBN 978-3-0343-0687-5

Vol. 137 Susy Macqueen
The Emergence of Patterns in Second Language Writing. A Sociocognitive Exploration of Lexical Trails.
325 pages. 2012. ISBN 978-3-0343-1010-9

Vol. 138 Maria Vittoria Calvi & Giovanna Mapelli (eds)
La lengua del turismo. Géneros discursivos y terminología.
365 pages. 2011. ISBN 978-3-0343-1011-6

Vol. 139 Ken Lau
Learning to Become a Professional in a Textually-Mediated World. A Text-Oriented Study of Placement Practices.
261 pages. 2012. ISBN 978-3-0343-1016-1

Vol. 140 Sandra Campagna, Giuliana Garzone, Cornelia Ilie & Elizabeth Rowley-Jolivet (eds)
Evolving Genres in Web-mediated Communication.
337 pages. 2012. ISBN 978-3-0343-1013-0

Vol. 141 Edith Esch & Martin Solly (eds)
The Sociolinguistics of Language Education in International Contexts.
263 pages. 2012. ISBN 978-3-0343-1009-3

Vol. 142 Forthcoming.

Vol. 143 David Tizón-Couto
Left Dislocation in English. A Functional-Discoursal Approach.
416 pages. 2012. ISBN 978-3-0343-1037-6

Vol. 144 Margrethe Petersen & Jan Engberg (eds)
Current Trends in LSP Research. Aims and Methods.
323 pages. 2011. ISBN 978-3-0343-1054-3

Vol. 145 David Tizón-Couto, Beatriz Tizón-Couto, Iria Pastor-Gómez & Paula Rodríguez-Puente (eds)
New Trends and Methodologies in Applied English Language Research II. Studies in Language Variation, Meaning and Learning.
283 pages. 2012. ISBN 978-3-0343-1061-1

Vol. 146 Rita Salvi & Hiromasa Tanaka (eds)
Intercultural Interactions in Business and Management.
306 pages. 2011. ISBN 978-3-0343-1039-0

Vol. 147 Francesco Straniero Sergio & Caterina Falbo (eds)
Breaking Ground in Corpus-based Interpreting Studies.
254 pages. 2012. ISBN 978-3-0343-1071-0

Vol. 148 Forthcoming.

Vol. 149 Vijay K. Bhatia & Paola Evangelisti Allori (eds)
Discourse and Identity in the Professions. Legal, Corporate and Institutional Citizenship.
352 pages. 2011. ISBN 978-3-0343-1079-6

Vol. 150 Maurizio Gotti (ed.)
Academic Identity Traits. A Corpus-Based Investigation.
363 pages. 2012. ISBN 978-3-0343-1141-0

Vol. 151 Priscilla Heynderickx, Sylvain Dieltjens, Geert Jacobs, Paul Gillaerts & Elizabeth de Groot (eds)
The Language Factor in International Business. New Perspectives on Research, Teaching and Practice.
320 pages. 2012. ISBN 978-3-0343-1090-1

Vol. 152 Paul Gillaerts, Elizabeth de Groot, Sylvain Dieltjens, Priscilla Heynderickx & Geert Jacobs (eds)
Researching Discourse in Business Genres. Cases and Corpora.
215 pages. 2012. ISBN 978-3-0343-1092-5

Vol. 153 Yongyan Zheng
Dynamic Vocabulary Development in a Foreign Language.
262 pages. 2012. ISBN 978-3-0343-1106-9

Vol. 154 Carmen Argondizzo (ed.)
Creativity and Innovation in Language Education.
357 pages. 2012. ISBN 978-3-0343-1080-2

Vol. 155 David Hirsh (ed.)
Current Perspectives in Second Language Vocabulary Research.
180 pages. 2012. ISBN 978-3-0343-1108-3

Vol. 156 Seiji Shinkawa
Unhistorical Gender Assignment in Lahamon's Brut. A Case Study of a Late Stage in the Development of Grammatical Gender toward its Ultimate Loss.
186 pages. 2012. ISBN 978-3-0343-1124-3

Vol. 157 Yeonkwon Jung
Basics of Organizational Writing: A Critical Reading Approach.
151 pages. 2014. ISBN 978-3-0343-1137-3.

Vol. 158 Bárbara Eizaga Rebollar (ed.)
Studies in Linguistics and Cognition.
301 pages. 2012. ISBN 978-3-0343-1138-0

Vol. 159 Giuliana Garzone, Paola Catenaccio, Chiara Degano (eds)
Genre Change in the Contemporary World. Short-term Diachronic Perspectives.
329 pages. 2012. ISBN 978-3-0343-1214-1

Vol. 160 Carol Berkenkotter, Vijay K. Bhatia & Maurizio Gotti (eds)
Insights into Academic Genres.
468 pages. 2012. ISBN 978-3-0343-1211-0

Vol. 161 Beatriz Tizón-Couto
Clausal Complements in Native and Learner Spoken English. A corpus-based study with Lindsei and Vicolse.
357 pages. 2013. ISBN 978-3-0343-1184-7

Vol. 162 Patrizia Anesa
Jury Trials and the Popularization of Legal Language. A Discourse Analytical Approach.
247 pages. 2012. ISBN 978-3-0343-1231-8

Vol. 163 David Hirsh
Endangered Languages, Knowledge Systems and Belief Systems.
153 pages. 2013. ISBN 978-3-0343-1232-5

Vol. 164 Eugenia Sainz (ed.)
De la estructura de la frase al tejido del discurso. Estudios contrastivos español/ italiano.
305 pages. 2014. ISBN 978-3-0343-1253-0

Vol. 165 Julia Bamford, Franca Poppi & Davide Mazzi (eds)
Space, Place and the Discursive Construction of Identity.
367 pages. 2014. ISBN 978-3-0343-1249-3

Vol. 166 Rita Salvi & Janet Bowker (eds)
Space, Time and the Construction of Identity. Discursive Indexicality in Cultural, Institutional and Professional Fields.
324 pages. 2013. ISBN 978-3-0343-1254-7

Vol. 167 Shunji Yamazaki & Robert Sigley (eds)
Approaching Language Variation through Corpora. A Festschrift in Honour of Toshio Saito.
421 pages. 2013. ISBN 978-3-0343-1264-6

Vol. 168 Franca Poppi
Global Interactions in English as a Lingua Franca. How written communication is changing under the influence of electronic media and new contexts of use.
249 pages. 2012. ISBN 978-3-0343-1276-9

Vol. 169 Miguel A. Aijón Oliva & María José Serrano
Style in syntax. Investigating variation in Spanish pronoun subjects.
239 pages. 2013. ISBN 978-3-0343-1244-8

Vol. 170 Inés Olza, Óscar Loureda & Manuel Casado-Velarde (eds)
Language Use in the Public Sphere. Methodological Perspectives and Empirical Applications.
564 pages. 2014. ISBN 978-3-0343-1286-8

Vol. 171 Aleksandra Matulewska
Legilinguistic Translatology. A Parametric Approach to Legal Translation.
279 pages. 2013. ISBN 978-3-0343-1287-5

Vol. 172 Maurizio Gotti & Carmen Sancho Guinda (eds)
Narratives in Academic and Professional Genres.
513 pages. 2013. ISBN 978-3-0343-1371-1

Vol. 173 Madalina Chitez
Learner corpus profiles. The case of Romanian Learner English.
244 pages. 2014. ISBN 978-3-0343-1410-7

Vol. 174 Chihiro Inoue
Task Equivalence in Speaking Tests.
251 pages. 2013. ISBN 978-3-0343-1417-6

Vol. 175 Gabriel Quiroz & Pedro Patiño (eds.)
LSP in Colombia: advances and challenges.
339 pages. 2014. ISBN 978-3-0343-1434-3

Vol. 176 Catherine Resche
Economic Terms and Beyond: Capitalising on the Wealth of Notions. How Researchers in Specialised Varieties of English Can Benefit from Focusing on Terms.
332 pages. 2013. ISBN 978-3-0343-1435-0

Vol. 177 Wei Wang
Media representation of migrant workers in China. Identities and stances.
198 pages. 2018. 978-3-0343-1436-7

Vol. 178 Cécile Desoutter & Caroline Mellet (dir.)
Le discours rapporté: approches linguistiques et perspectives didactiques.
270 pages. 2013. ISBN 978-3-0343-1292-9

Vol. 179 Ana Díaz-Negrillo & Francisco Javier Díaz-Pérez (eds)
Specialisation and Variation in Language Corpora.
341 pages. 2014. ISBN 978-3-0343-1316-2

Vol. 180 Pilar Alonso
A Multi-dimensional Approach to Discourse Coherence. From Standardness to Creativity.
247 pages. 2014. ISBN 978-3-0343-1325-4

Vol. 181 Alejandro Alcaraz-Sintes & Salvador Valera-Hernández (eds)
Diachrony and Synchrony in English Corpus Linguistics.
393 pages. 2014. ISBN 978-3-0343-1326-1

Vol. 182 Runhan Zhang
Investigating Linguistic Knowledge of a Second Language.
207 pages. 2015. ISBN 978-3-0343-1330-8

Vol. 183 Hajar Abdul Rahim & Shakila Abdul Manan (eds.)
English in Malaysia. Postcolonial and Beyond.
267 pages. 2014. ISBN 978-3-0343-1341-4

Vol. 184 Virginie Fasel Lauzon
Comprendre et apprendre dans l'interaction. Les séquences d'explication en classe de français langue seconde.
292 pages. 2014. ISBN 978-3-0343-1451-0

Vol. 185 Forthcoming.

Vol. 186 Wei Ren
L2 Pragmatic Development in Study Abroad Contexts.
256 pages. 2015. ISBN 978-3-0343-1358-2

Vol. 187 Marina Bondi & Rosa Lorés Sanz (eds)
Abstracts in Academic Discourse. Variation and Change.
361 pages. 2014. ISBN 978-3-0343-1483-1

Vol. 188 Giuditta Caliendo
Rethinking Community. Discourse, Identity and Citizenship in the European Union.
240 pages. 2017. ISBN 978-3-0343-1561-6

Vol. 189 Paola Evangelisti Allori (ed.)
Identities in and across Cultures.
315 pages. 2014. ISBN 978-3-0343-1458-9

Vol. 190 Erik Castello, Katherine Ackerley & Francesca Coccetta (eds).
Studies in Learner Corpus Linguistics. Research and Applications for Foreign Language Teaching and Assessment.
358 pages. 2015. ISBN 978-3-0343-1506-7

Vol. 191 Ruth Breeze, Maurizio Gotti & Carmen Sancho Guinda (eds)
Interpersonality in Legal Genres.
389 pages. 2014. ISBN 978-3-0343-1524-1

Vol. 192 Paola Evangelisti Allori, John Bateman & Vijay K. Bhatia (eds)
Evolution in Genre. Emergence, Variation, Multimodality.
364 pages. 2014. ISBN 978-3-0343-1533-3

Vol. 193 Jiyeon Kook
Agency in Arzt-Patient-Gesprächen. Zur interaktionistischen Konzeptualisierung von Agency.
271 pages. 2015. ISBN 978-3-0343-1666-8

Vol. 194 Susana Nicolás Román & Juan José Torres Núñez (eds)
Drama and CLIL. A new challenge for the teaching approaches in bilingual education.
170 pages. 2015. ISBN 978-3-0343-1629-3

Vol. 195 Alessandra Molino & Serenella Zanotti (eds)
Observing Norm, Observing Usage. Lexis in Dictionaries and in the Media.
430 pages. 2015. ISBN 978-3-0343-1584-5

Vol. 196 Begoña Soneira
A Lexical Description of English for Architecture. A Corpus-based Approach.
267 pages. 2015. ISBN 978-3-0343-1602-6

Vol. 197 M Luisa Roca-Varela
False Friends in Learner Corpora. A corpus-based study of English false friends in the written and spoken production of Spanish learners.
348 pages. 2015. ISBN 978-3-0343-1620-0

Vol. 198 Rahma Al-Mahrooqi & Christopher Denman
Bridging the Gap between Education and Employment. English Language Instruction in EFL Contexts.
416 pages. 2015. ISBN 978-3-0343-1681-1

Vol. 199 Rita Salvi & Janet Bowker (eds)
The Dissemination of Contemporary Knowledge in English. Genres, discourse strategies and professional practices.
171 pages. 2015. ISBN 978-3-0343-1679-8

Vol. 200 Maurizio Gotti & Davide S. Giannoni (eds)
Corpus Analysis for Descriptive and Pedagogical Purposes. ESP Perspectives.
432 pages. 2014. ISBN 978-3-0343-1516-6

Vol. 201 Ida Ruffolo
The Perception of Nature in Travel Promotion Texts. A Corpus-based Discourse Analysis.
148 pages. 2015. ISBN 978-3-0343-1521-0

Vol. 202 Ives Trevian
English suffixes. Stress-assignment properties, productivity, selection and combinatorial processes.
471 pages. 2015. ISBN 978-3-0343-1576-0

Vol. 203 Maurizio Gotti, Stefania Maci & Michele Sala (eds)
Insights into Medical Communication.
422 pages. 2015. ISBN 978-3-0343-1694-1

Vol. 204 Carmen Argondizzo (ed.)
European Projects in University Language Centres. Creativity, Dynamics, Best Practice.
371 pages. 2015. ISBN 978-3-0343-1696-5

Vol. 205 Aura Luz Duffé Montalván (ed.)
Estudios sobre el léxico. Puntos y contrapuntos.
502 pages. 2016. ISBN 978-3-0343-2011-5

Vol. 206 Maria Pavesi, Maicol Formentelli & Elisa Ghia (eds)
The Languages of Dubbing. Mainstream Audiovisual Translation in Italy.
275 pages. 2014. ISBN 978-3-0343-1646-0

Vol. 207 Ruth Breeze & Inés Olza (eds)
Evaluation in media discourse. European perspectives.
268 pages. 2017. ISBN 978-3-0343-2014-6

Vol. 208 Vijay K. Bhatia & Maurizio Gotti (eds)
Arbitration Discourse in Asia.
331 pages. 2015. ISBN 978-3-0343-2032-0

Vol. 209 Sofía Bemposta-Rivas, Carla Bouzada-Jabois, Yolanda Fernández-Pena, Tamara Bouso, Yolanda J. Calvo-Benzies, Iván Tamaredo (eds)
New trends and methodologies in applied English language research III. Synchronic and diachronic studies on discourse, lexis and grammar processing.
280 pages. 2017. ISBN 978-3-0343-2039-9

Vol. 210 Francisco Alonso Almeida, Laura Cruz García & Víctor González Ruiz (eds)
Corpus-based studies on language varieties.
285 pages. 2016. ISBN 978-3-0343-2044-3

Vol. 211 Juan Pedro Rica Peromingo
Aspectos lingüísticos y técnicos de la traducción audiovisual (TAV).
177 pages. 2016. ISBN 978-3-0343-2055-9

Vol. 212 Maria Vender
Disentangling Dyslexia. Phonological and Processing Deficit in Developmental Dyslexia.
338 pages. 2017. ISBN 978-3-0343-2064-1

Vol. 213 Zhilong Xie
Bilingual Advantages. Contributions of Different Bilingual Experiences to Cognitive Control Differences Among Young-adult Bilinguals.
221 pages. 2016. ISBN 978-3-0343-2081-8

Vol. 214 Larissa D'Angelo
Academic posters. A textual and visual metadiscourse analysis.
367 pages. 2016. ISBN 978-3-0343-2083-2

Vol. 215 Evelyne Berger
Prendre la parole en L2. Regard sur la compétence d'interaction en classe de langue.
246 pages. 2016. ISBN 978-3-0343-2084-9

Vol. 216 David Lasagabaster and Aintzane Doiz (eds)
CLIL experiences in secondary and tertiary education: In search of good practices.
262 pages. 2016. ISBN 978-3-0343-2104-4

Vol. 217 Elena Kkese
Identifying Plosives in L2 English: The Case of L1 Cypriot Greek Speakers.
317 pages. 2016. ISBN 978-3-0343-2060-3

Vol. 218 Sandra Campagna, Elana Ochse, Virginia Pulcini & Martin Solly (eds)
Languaging in and across Communities: New Voices, New Identities. Studies in Honour of Giuseppina Cortese.
507 pages. 2016. ISBN 978-3-0343-2073-3

Vol. 219 Adriana Orlandi & Laura Giacomini (ed.)
Defining collocation for lexicographic purposes. From linguistic theory to lexicographic practice.
328 pages. 2016. ISBN 978-3-0343-2054-2

Vol. 220 Pietro Luigi Iaia
Analysing English as a Lingua Franca in Video Games. Linguistic Features, Experiential and Functional Dimensions of Online and Scripted Interactions.
139 pages. 2016. ISBN 978-3-0343-2138-9

Vol. 221 Dimitrinka G. Níkleva (ed.)
La formación de los docentes de español para inmigrantes en distintos contextos educativos.
390 pages. 2017. ISBN 978-3-0343-2135-8

Vol. 222 Katherine Ackerley, Marta Guarda & Francesca Helm (eds)
Sharing Perspectives on English-Medium Instruction.
308 pages. 2017. ISBN 978-3-0343-2537-0

Vol. 223 Juana I. Marín-Arrese, Julia Lavid-López, Marta Carretero, Elena Domínguez Romero, Mª Victoria Martín de la Rosa & María Pérez Blanco (eds)
Evidentiality and Modality in European Languages. Discourse-pragmatic perspectives.
427 pages. 2017. ISBN 978-3-0343-2437-3

Vol. 224 Gilles Col
Construction du sens : un modèle instructionnel pour la sémantique.
292 pages. 2017. ISBN 978-3-0343-2572-1

Vol. 225 Ana Chiquito & Gabriel Quiroz (eds)
Pobreza, Lenguaje y Medios en América Latina.
362 pages. 2017. ISBN 978-3-0343-2142-6

Vol. 226 Xu Zhang
English Quasi-Numeral Classifiers. A Corpus-Based Cognitive-Typological Study.
360 pages. 2017. ISBN 978-3-0343-2818-0

Vol. 227 María Ángeles Orts, Ruth Breeze & Maurizio Gotti (eds)
Power, Persuasion and Manipulation in Specialised Genres. Providing Keys to the Rhetoric of Professional Communities.
368 pages. 2017. ISBN 978-3-0343-3010-7

Vol. 228 Maurizio Gotti, Stefania Maci & Michele Sala (eds)
Ways of Seeing, Ways of Being: Representing the Voices of Tourism.
453 pages. 2017. ISBN 978-3-0343-3031-2

Vol. 229 Dino Selvaggi
Plurilingual Code-Switching between Standard and Local Varieties. A Socio-Psycholinguistic Approach.
371 pages. 2018. ISBN 978-3-0343-2663-6

Vol. 230 Anca-Cristina Sterie
Interprofessional interactions at the hospital. Nurses' requests and reports of problems in calls with physicians.
371 pages. 2017. ISBN 978-3-0343-2734-3

Vol. 231 Xiaodong Zhang
Understanding Chinese EFL Teachers' Beliefs and Practices in the Textbook-Based Classroom.
189 pages. 2017. ISBN 978-3-0343-3053-4

Vol. 232 Manuela Caterina Moroni & Federica Ricci Garotti (Hrsg.)
Brücken schlagen zwischen Sprachwissenschaft und DaF-Didaktik.
345 pages. 2017. ISBN 978-3-0343-2667-4

Vol. 233 Dimitrinka Georgieva Níkleva
Necesidades y tendencias en la formación del profesorado de español como lengua extranjera.
401 pages. 2017. ISBN 978-3-0343-2946-0

Vol. 234 Juan Santana-Lario & Salvador Valera (Hrsg.)
Competing patterns in English affixation.
272 pages. 2017. ISBN 978-3-0343-2701-5

Vol. 235 Francisco Salgado-Robles
Desarrollo de la competencia sociolingüística por aprendices de español en un contexto de inmersión en el extranjero.
241 pages. 2018. ISBN 978-3-0343-2323-9

Vol. 236 Maria Chiara Janner
Sguardi linguistici sulla marca. Analisi morfosintattica dei nomi commerciali in italiano.
345 pages. 2017. ISBN 978-3-0343-2667-4

Vol. 237 Bárbara Herrero Muñoz-Cobo & Otman El Azami Zalachi
La primavera del árabe marroquí.
192 pages. 2017. ISBN 978-3-0343-3104-3

Vol. 238 Consuelo Pascual Escagedo
El papel del oyente en la construcción de la conversación espontánea de estudiantes italianos en su interlengua y en su lengua materna.
295 pages. 2017. ISBN 978-3-0343-3186-9

Vol. 239 Stefania M. Maci
The MS Digby 133 Mary Magdalene. Beyond scribal practices: language, discourse, values and attitudes.
336 pages. 2017. ISBN 978-3-0343-3256-9

Vol. 240 Eliecer Crespo-Fernández
Taboo in Discourse. Studies on Attenuation and Offence in Communication.
326 pages. 2018. ISBN 978-3-0343-3018-3

Vol. 241 Jana Altmanova, Maria Centrella, Katherine E. Russo (eds)
Terminology & Discourse / Terminologie et discours.
424 pages. 2018. ISBN 978-3-0343-2417-5

Vol. 242 Xavier Blanco et Inès Sfar (dir.)
Lexicologie(s) : approches croisées en sémantique lexicale.
442 pages. 2018. ISBN 978-3-0343-3056-5

Vol. 243 Yunfeng Ge
Resolution of Conflict of Interest in Chinese Civil Court Hearings. A Perspective of Discourse Information Theory.
302 pages. 2018. ISBN 978-3-0343-3313-9

Vol. 244 Carla Vergaro
Illocutionary Shell Nouns in English.
322 pages. 2018. ISBN 978-3-0343-3069-5

Vol. 245 Paolo Frassi
L'adjectif en français et sa définition lexicographique.
270 pages. 2018. ISBN 978-3-0343-3394-8

Vol. 246 Suwilai Premsrirat and David Hirsh (eds)
Language Revitalization. Insights from Thailand.
328 pages. 2018. ISBN 978-3-0343-3497-6

Vol. 247 Wei Wang
Researching Learning and Learners in Genre-based Academic Writing Instruction.
282 pages. 2018. ISBN 978-3-0343-3297-2

Vol. 248 Isusi Alabarte, Alberto & Lahuerta Martínez, Ana Cristina (eds)
La comprensión lectora de lengua extranjera. Estudio de los factores de familiaridad, interés, género y métodos de evaluación.
336 pages. 2018. ISBN 978-3-0343-3493-8

Vol. 249 Mercedes Eurrutia Cavero
Approche didactique du langage techno-scientifique Terminologie et discours.
374 pages. 2018. ISBN 978-3-0343-3512-6

Vol. 250 Aurora Ruiz Mezcua (ed.)
Approaches to Telephone Interpretation Research, Innovation, Teaching and Transference.
268 pages. 2018. ISBN 978-3-0343-3330-6

Vol. 251 Morini Massimiliano
A Day in the News A Stylistic Analysis of Newsspeak.
188 pages. 2018. ISBN 978-3-0343-3507-2

Vol. 252 Ignacio Guillén-Galve & Ignacio Vázquez-Orta (eds.)
English as a Lingua Franca and Intercultural Communication Implications and Applications in the Field of English Language Teaching.
414 pages. 2018. ISBN 978-3-0343-2763-3

Vol. 253 Bianca Del Villano
Using the Devil with Courtesy. Shakespeare and the Language of (Im)Politeness.
216 pages. 2018. ISBN 978-3-0343-2315-4

Vol. 254 David Hirsh (ed.)
Explorations in Second Language Vocabulary Research.
252 pages. 2018. ISBN 978-3-0343-2940-8

Vol. 255 Tania Baumann (ed.)
Reiseführer - Sprach- und Kulturmittlung im Tourismus / Le guide turistiche - mediazione linguistica e culturale in ambito turistico.
270 pages. 2018. ISBN 978-3-0343-3402-0

Vol. 256 Ariadna Sánchez-Hernández & Ana Herraiz-Martínez (eds)
Learning second language pragmatics beyond traditional contexts.
376 pages. 2018. ISBN 978-3-0343-3437-2

Vol. 257 Albert Bastardas-Boada, Emili Boix-Fuster, Rosa Maria Torrens (eds)
Family Multilingualism in Medium-Sized Linguistic Communities.
336 pages. 2019. ISBN 978-3-0343-2536-3

Vol. 258 Yuyang Cai
Examining the Interaction among Components of English for Specific Purposes Ability in Reading. The Triple-Decker Model.
296 pages. 2020. 978-3-0343-2913-2

Vol. 259 Catia Nannoni
Participe présent et gérondif dans la presse française contemporaine.
176 pages. 2019. ISBN 978-3-0343-3631-4

Vol. 260 Nieves Rodríguez Pérez & Bárbara Heinsch (eds.)
Contextos multilingües. Mediadores interculturales, formación del profesorado de lenguas extranjeras.
289 pages. 2019. ISBN 978-3-0343-3768-7

Vol. 261 Giuliana Elena Garzone, Mara Logaldo, Francesca Santulli (eds.)
Investigating Conflict Discourses in the Periodical Press.
244 pages. 2020. ISBN 978-3-0343-3668-0

Vol. 262 Laura Nadal
Lingüística experimental y contraargumentación.
233 pages. 2019. ISBN 978-3-0343-3791-5

Vol. 263 Claudia Claridge & Merja Kytö (eds.)
Punctuation in Context – Past and Present Perspectives.
288 pages. 2019. ISBN 978-3-0343-3790-8

Vol. 264 Maurizio Gotti, Stefania Maci, Michele Sala (eds.)
Scholarly Pathways.
530 pages. 2020. ISBN 978-3-0343-3860-8

Vol. 265 Ruth Breeze, Ana M. Fernández Vallejo (eds.)
Politics and populism across modes and media.
350 pages. 2020. ISBN 978-3-0343-3707-6

Vol. 266 Jean Marguerite Jimenez
Understanding the Effects of Immediate Electronic Corrective Feedback on Second Language Development.
252 pages. 2020. ISBN 978-3-0343-3815-8

Vol. 267 Sergio Rodríguez-Tapia, Adela González-Fernández (eds)
Lenguas y turismo: estudios en torno al discurso, la didáctica y la divulgación.
380 pages. 2020. ISBN 978-3-0343-3881-3

Vol. 268 Ana Bocanegra-Valle (ed.)
Applied Linguistics and Knowledge Transfer. Employability, Internationalisation and Social Challenges.
344 pages. 2020. ISBN 978-3-0343-3714-4

Vol. 269 Beatrice Garzelli
La traducción audiovisual español-italiano.Películas y cortos entre humor y habla soez.
202 pages. 2020. ISBN 978-3-0343-4013-7

Vol. 270 Iván Tamaredo
Complexity, Efficiency, and Language Contact. Pronoun Omission in World Englishes.
292 pages. 2020. ISBN 978-3-0343-3902-5

Vol. 271 Silvia Domenica Zollo
Origine et histoire du vocabulaire des arts de la table. Analyse lexicale et exploitation de corpus textuels.
239 pages. 2020. ISBN 978-3-0343-3890-5

Vol. 272 Paola Paissa, Michelangelo Conoscenti, Ruggero Druetta, Martin Solly (eds.)
Metaphor and Conflict / Métaphore et conflit.
385 pages. 2021. 978-3-0343-4068-7

Vol. 273 María Martínez-Atienza de Dios
Entre el léxico y la sintaxis: las fases de los eventos.
178 pages. 2021. 978-3-0343-4173-8

Vol. 274 Noelia Castro-Chao
Argument Structure in Flux. The Development of Impersonal Constructions in Middle and Early Modern English, with Special Reference to Verbs of Desire.
300 pages. 2021. 978-3-0343-4189-9

Vol. 275 Gabriella Carobbio, Cécile Desoutter, Aurora Fragonara (eds.)
Macht, Ratio und Emotion: Diskurse im digitalen Zeitalter / Pouvoir, raison et émotion: les discours à l'ère du numérique.
246 pages. 2020. 978-3-0343-4184-4

Vol. 276 Miguel Fuster-Márquez, José Santaemilia, Carmen Gregori-Signes, Paula Rodríguez-Abruñeiras (eds.)
Exploring discourse and ideology through corpora.
293 pages. 2021. 978-3-0343-3969-8

Vol. 277 Tamara Bouso
Changes in Argument Structure The Transitivizing Reaction Object Construction.
392 pages. 2021. 978-3-0343-4095-3

Vol. 278 Maria Luisa Maggioni, Amanda Murphy (eds.)
Back to the Future. English from Past to Present.
250 pages. 2021. 978-3-0343-4273-5

Vol. 279 Luisa Chierichetti
Diálogos de serie. Una aproximación a la construcción discursiva de personajes basada en corpus.
246 pages. 2021. 978-3-0343-4274-2

Vol. 280 Cristina Lastres-López
From subordination to insubordination. A functional-pragmatic approach to if/ si-constructions in English, French and Spanish spoken discourse.
258 pages. 2021. 978-3-0343-4220-9

Vol. 281 Eleonora Federici, Stefania Maci (eds.)
Gender issues. Translating and mediating languages, cultures and societies.
500 pages. 2021. 978-3-0343-4022-9

Vol. 282 José Mateo, Francisco Yus (eds.)
Metaphor in Economics and specialised Discourse.
354 pages. 2021. 978-3-0343-4048-9

Vol. 283 Nicholas Brownlees (ed.)
The Role of Context in the Production and Reception of Historical News Discourse.
376 pages. 2021. 978-3-0343-4181-3

Vol. 284 Catalina Fuentes Rodriguez, María Ester Brenes Peña, Víctor Pérez Béjar (eds.)
Sintaxis discursiva: construcciones y operadores en español.
396 pages. 2021. 978-3-0343-4306-0

Vol. 285 Dominic Stewart
Frequency in the dictionary. A corpus-assisted contrastive analysis of English and Italian.
178 pages. 2021. 978-3-0343-4368-8

Vol. 286 Carla Bouzada-Jabois
Nonfinite supplements in the recent history of English.
386 pages. 2021. 978-3-0343-4226-1

Vol. 287 Sofía Bemposta Rivas
Verb-governed infinitival complementation in the recent history of English.
340 pages. 2021. 978-3-0343-4227-8

Vol. 288 Mirella Agorni
Translating Italy for the Nineteenth Century. Translators and an Imagined Nation in the Early Romantic Period 1816–1830s.
182 pages. 2021. 978-3-0343-3612-3

Vol. 289 David Hirsh (ed.)
Research Perspectives in Language and Education.
276 pages. 2021. 978-3-0343-4219-3

Vol. 290 Federica Vezzani
Terminologie numérique : conception, représentation et gestion.
238 pages. 2022. 978-3-0343-4394-7

Vol. 291 Stefania M. Maci
Evidential verbs in the genre of medical posters. A corpus-based analysis.
498 pages. 2022. 978-3-0343-4521-7

Vol. 292 Francisco J. Álvarez-Gil
Stance devices in tourism-related research articles: A corpus-based study.
170 pages. 2022. 978-3-0343-4555-2

Vol. 293 Annalisa Baicchi / Stefania Biscetti (eds.)
The Language of Fashion. Linguistic, Cognitive, and Cultural Insights.
192 pages. 2022. 978-3-0343-4428-9

Vol. 294 Ana Maria Piquer-Píriz
E-learning in EMI. Academic language for university students.
228 pages. 2022. 978-3-0343-4589-7

Vol. 295 Geneviève Henrot Sostero (ed.)
Alle radici della fraseologia europea.
638 pages. 2023. 978-3-0343-4645-0

Vol. 296 Klara Dankova
Les fibres textiles entre synchronie et diachronie: études terminologiques.
288 pages. 2023. 978-3-0343-4587-3

Vol. 297 Marta Carretero, Juana I. Marín-Arrese, Elena Domínguez Romero, Mª Victoria Martín de la Rosa (eds.)
Evidentiality and Epistemic Modality. Conceptual and Descriptive issues.
414 pages. 2023. 978-3-0343-3993-3

Vol. 298 Kim Grego, Alessandra Vicentini, Virpi Ylänne (eds.)
Age-Specific Issues. Language, Spaces, Technologies.
280 pages. 2023. 978-3-0343-4411-1

Vol. 299 Giovanni Garofalo (ed.)
Estudios de género asistidos por corpus. Enfoques multidisciplinarios.
290 pages. 2022. 978-3-0343-4548-4

Vol. 300 Giuseppe Palumbo, Katia Peruzzo, Gianluca Pontrandolfo (eds.)
What's Special About Specialised Translation? Essays in Honour of Federica Scarpa.
298 pages. 2023. 978-3-0343-4411-1

Vol. 301 Raquel P. Romasanta
Probabilistic variability in clausal verb complementation in World Englishes.
374 pages. 2023. 978-3-0343-4703-7

Vol. 302 Giulia Adriana Pennisi
A linguistic Insight into Legislative Drafting. Tradition and Change in the UK Legislation.
296 pages. 2023. 978-3-0343-4700-6

Vol. 303 Javier Fernández-Cruz, Antonio Moreno-Ortiz
Economic terms in the news during the Great Recession. A diachronic sentiment and collocational analysis.
192 pages. 2023. 978-3-0343-4778-5

Vol. 304 Stefania Maci, Mark McGlashan (eds.)
(Critical) Discourse Studies and the (new?) normal. Analysing discourse in times of crisis.
400 pages. 2024. 978-3-0343-4767-9

Vol. 305 Ana Elvira Ojanguren López
Predications in competition and the rise of serial verb constructions in English. The verbal and nominal complementation of Old English aspectual and manipulative verbs.
534 pages. 2024. 978-3-0343-4644-3

Vol. 306 Stefania Maci, Giovanni Garofalo (eds.)
Investigating Discourse and Text. Corpus-Assisted Analytical Perspectives.
372 pages. 2023. 978-3-0343-4753-2

Vol. 307 Víctor Pérez Béjar
Las construcciones suspendidas en español. Un paradigma en gramática del discurso.
494 pages. 2024. 978-3-0343-4799-0

Vol. 308 Javier Calle Martín / Jeús Romero Barranco (eds.)
Corpora and Language Change in Late Modern English.
408 pages. 2024. 978-3-0343-4642-9

Vol. 309 Cristina Petras / Sonia Berbinski / Daciana Vlad / Raluca Balaţchi (eds.)
Marqueurs métalinguistiques : émergence, discours, variation / Metalinguistic Markers: Emergence, Discourse, Variation.
720 pages. 2024. 978-3-0343-4908-6

Vol. 310 Micaela Rossi (éd.)
Néologie, terminologie et variation - Neología, terminología yvariación – Neologia, terminologia e variazione.
418 Pages. 2024. 978-3-0343-4696-2

Vol. 311 Sergio Maruenda-Bataller / Laura Mercé / Elena Castellano-Ortolà (eds.)
Discourse, gender, and violence: Insights from news and social media texts.
268 pages. 2024. 978-3-0343-4701-3

Vol. 312 Dario Del Fante
Migrating across times and cultures: Metaphorical images of migration in the U.S. and Italian newspaper discourse between the 20th and 21st centuries.
338 Pages. 2024. 978-3-0343-4659-7

Vol. 313 Begoña Bellés-Fortuño / Francisco Alonso Almeida (eds.)
Corpus-based Studies in Specialized Discourses.
294 Pages. 2025. 978-3-0343-4261-2

Vol. 314 Elaine Millar
Multi-word Verbs in English Language Teaching: Insights from research and practice.
252 Pages. 2025. 978-3-0343-5441-7

Vol. 315 Irene Guzmán-Alcón / Richard Nightingale (eds.)
New Directions in Instructional Pragmatics Research.
424 pages. 2025. 978-3-0343-5099-0

Vol. 316 Rosa Rabadán / Noelia Ramón (eds.)
Cross-linguistic Mediated Communication: Hybrid Text Production English-Spanish.
282 pages. 2025. 978-3-0343-5100-3

Vol. 317 Alba E. Ruz
Directionality in English morphological conversion.
214 pages. 2025. 978-3-0343-5788-3

Vol. 318 David Hirsh
Lexical Profile of AI-Generated Content in Higher Education.
200 pages. 2025. 978-3-0343-6113-2

www.ingramcontent.com/pod-product-compliance
Ingram Content Group UK Ltd.
Pitfield, Milton Keynes, MK11 3LW, UK
UKHW021839100926
8556IPUK00004B/430